"Weaving personal experience and biblical truth, my friend Jim Daly offers hope to all those who have yearned for the belonging, the love, and the shelter that the word *home* should evoke. Whether you are a struggling parent trying to create a good environment for your family, or a grown child still longing for a home you never knew, Daly's excellent book offers a roadmap to the God who made His home among us."

—CHUCK COLSON, FOUNDER, PRISON FELLOWSHIP

"Ever felt broken? Ever longed for home? Jim Daly has a powerful, fascinating story that will encourage your heart. He is a living example of someone who has used his pain to become better, not bitter and is being used by God to change the world. Prepare to be inspired!"

—REBECCA ST. JAMES, GRAMMY AWARD–WINNING CHRISTIAN
SINGER/BEST-SELLING AUTHOR

"A true story of God's redemption."

—JASON ELAM, DENVER BRONCOS NFL FRANCHISE KICKER

"Jim Daly's book had a huge impact on me. This is a powerful story of a kid who lived in twenty-four houses by the age of eighteen yet never lost hope that life would be better, that God had a plan for his life. And what a plan! The pain of Jim's youth has been transformed into a passion for strengthening and saving others from the heartache he experienced. It is such an encouragement to see how God takes our hardships and uses them to create something beautiful if we will only let Him."

—SHAUNTI FELDHAHN, BEST-SELLING AUTHOR, *FOR WOMEN ONLY: WHAT
YOU NEED TO KNOW ABOUT THE INNER LIVES OF MEN*,
PUBLIC SPEAKER, AND NEWSPAPER COLUMNIST

"From a broken family to a champion for families, Jim Daly demonstrates how God can use the broken hearted to accomplish great things in His kingdom. Anyone with scars from their own childhood will find great encouragement in Jim's compelling story."

—RICH STEARNS, PRESIDENT, WORLD VISION US

"Jim Daly has done a beautiful job of reminding us that God is involved in the details of our lives. Through his personal journey, we see that there is purpose in our pain. Thank you, Mr. Daly, for your transparency."

—NATALIE GRANT, AWARD WINNING SINGER/SONGWRITER

"Need encouragement, help, and significance in your life? You'll find it in Jim Daly's book *Finding Home.*"

—DR. KEVIN LEMAN, AUTHOR,
*MAKING CHILDREN MIND WITHOUT LOSING YOURS*

"This is possibly the most inspiring story of growing up and finding God that I have heard in my short fifteen years. *Finding Home* is one of those books that bridges gaps between generations and helps us all appreciate the lengths God will go to in order to prove that in His family, there are no orphans.

"No matter what you're facing in life God is bigger. Jim Daly's story proves that. Jim Daly's story offers hope to young people who feel like they have been abandoned and wonder if God really has a plan for them."

—ZACH HUNTER, 15, AUTHOR, *BE THE CHANGE*,
FOUNDER, LOOSE CHANGE TO LOOSEN CHAINS

"For many years our family has enjoyed the ministry of Focus on the Family. I'm delighted to see Jim leading the organization. His story will shock, encourage, challenge, and inspire you."

—Pat Gelsinger, senior VP Intel Corp.,
author, *Balancing Family Faith & Work*

"Jim has written from the heart and shares his experiences with honest and sincerity. His story is one I relate to as I, too, grew up apart from a father's love and devotion. Because of God's grace, Jim encourages us to pursue better marriages, better families, better life experiences, and better lives. He never comes off sounding like he knows it all; instead he comes across as a friend offering a warm cup of coffee, a smile, and a tender heart."

—Steve Largent, former NFL player,
member of United States Congress

"What a wonderful insight into a man who is devoting his life to improving the family!"

—Dean C. Borgman, chairman (ret.), Sikorsky Aircraft Corp.

"Jim's story shows us how God quiets storms in our lives and gives our lives new meaning. *Finding Home* is a must read!"

—Harry R. Jackson, Jr., senior pastor, Hope Christian Church,
founder, High Impact Leadership Coalition

"Jim's compelling story will grip you from the first page. He offers many lessons on how faith helped him overcome a very dysfunctional childhood. Thank you, Jim, for opening up your life to us."

—Mac McQuiston, CEO, Forum, Inc.

"Jim Daly paints a very clear picture of some of the challenges kids face in broken and abusive homes today. The heart-wrenching truths you find in his story portray the beauty of healing and restoration that comes when we are recklessly abandoned to God."

—RON LUCE, PRESIDENT AND FOUNDER, TEEN MANIA MINISTRIES

"Jim Daly has revealed his life story in collections of humor, great pain, difficulty, and sometimes odd experiences that put him in the position for God to be able to do great works through him. Readers will be blessed."

—MATTHEW K. ROSE, CHAIRMAN, BNSF RAILWAY

# Finding Home

## An Imperfect Path to Faith and Family

# JIM DALY

WITH BOB DEMOSS

David C Cook®

*transforming lives together*

FINDING HOME
Published by David C. Cook
4050 Lee Vance View
Colorado Springs, CO 80918 U.S.A.

David C. Cook Distribution Canada
55 Woodslee Avenue, Paris, Ontario, Canada N3L 3E5

David C. Cook U.K., Kingsway Communications
Eastbourne, East Sussex BN23 6NT, England

Scripture quotations are taken from the *Holy Bible, New International Version*®. *NIV*®.
Copyright 1973, 1978, 1984 by International Bible Society. Used by permission of
Zondervan. All rights reserved.

"Cry Out to Jesus" by Tai Anderson, Mark Lee, Mac Powell, David Carr, and Brad Avery.
Copyright © 2005 Consuming Fire Music (ASCAP) (adm. by EMI CMG Publishing).
All rights reserved. Used by permission.

All names in this book are taken from the author's memory.
None have been intentionally changed.

LCCN 2007930615

ISBN 978-0-7814-4866-6

Jim Daly is represented by the literary agency of WordServe Literary Group,
10152 Knoll Circle, Highlands Ranch, CO 80130 (www.wordserveliterary.com).

Cover Design: The DesignWorks Group
Cover Photos: © DigitalVision/Getty Images; © Stephen Swintek/Getty Images
Interior Design: Karen Athen
Interior Photo Design: Ron Adair

Printed in the United States of America
First Edition 2007

1 2 3 4 5 6 7 8 9 10

061407

*To my mom for all the lessons about life ...*


*And to my family, Jean, Trent, and Troy,*
*with whom I'm finally home.*

# Contents

# Author's Note

Life is wonderful.

Life is hard.

I've experienced my share of both and prefer the good stuff this journey has to offer. Especially considering the train wreck that was characteristic of my childhood. As you'll soon discover, my family put the "D" into Dysfunction. My father stepped out of our cozy home when I was five. Then, at age nine, my mom died. Suddenly, I became an orphan.

I've had a few train wrecks.

I've had some major high points, too.

But in the end, I don't get to pick the events that impact my life. I have no control over such things. This I do know: How I respond to what comes my way will either make or break me. Kill me, or give me strength.

In the pages ahead I'm going to be open about my unusual path to finding faith and family. As you read, my sense is that God might just beckon you to embrace the story that is uniquely yours to tell, and to realize that, in spite of how things may appear at any given moment along the path, He has designed you to do something significant.

# 1

## Message in a Bottle

There's so much about that night I don't recall. If pressed for details, I couldn't tell you about the murder weapon. Was the instrument of death a shotgun or a knife? A baseball bat or a club? I just don't know. A set of brass knuckles can do real damage, I've been told, but I never learned what went down for certain.

Although I never heard a shot, the word on the street was that a shotgun had been used. My best guess is that the killing was gang related. Perhaps a little payback in the decades-old turf war between the Crips and the Bloods for control of illegal drugs. Or, it might have been a clash between the Latino gang element, the Hells Angels, and an African American posse in our racially mixed neighborhood.

You'll have to forgive me for being sketchy.

I was only eight at the time.

There are two unmistakable images forever imprinted on my mind. First, the yellow chalk line scratched onto the pavement outlining the position where the body fell in the alley. Second, the blood stain—a brownish-red calling card left behind by the victim for the rain to deal with. My memory of those two images is clear because the murder occurred about ten feet outside of my bedroom window … a real-life nightmare worse than any dream I'd ever had. Talk about inflaming the imagination of a child—no wonder I was afraid of the dark.

We were living in Compton at the time. Yes, *the* Compton—that concrete jungle of southeast Los Angeles popularized by rappers on MTV. Compton was, and still is, a rough place, no question about it. Drive-by shootings, crime, poverty, and vice were a way of life. For years Compton had the dubious distinction of being ranked as one of the highest crime cities in all of California.

And now we called Compton *home*.

Given the grave reputation of the city, I wasn't entirely surprised to discover our apartment had served as the backdrop for a homicide. And yet, let's just say it was a bit much for me, as a child, to process. I mean, the wall separating me from that savage deed was a mere four inches thick. I wondered how often this sort of thing happened in my new neighborhood. What if a more powerful gun was used the next time? A bullet could easily penetrate the thin layer of white stucco, make mincemeat of the flimsy drywall, and plow into my chest while I was sleeping.

Suddenly, my ground-floor bedroom, at the back of a two-story apartment complex and adjacent to a dark alley, made me feel exposed.

Vulnerable.

Defenseless.

In midspring of 1970, my stepfather, Hank, and my mom, Jan Daly, had moved the family from the rolling hills of Yucca Valley, California, to the gritty streets of Compton to save a little money. I knew their goal was to eventually move to the serene ocean-side community of Long Beach, California, but that came at a price I wasn't sure we ought to pay. But hey, I was a kid. My vote didn't count. And so the wail of sirens replaced the song of birds.

Not only was Compton a dangerous place, it was *noisy*. Not a happy noisy like the sound of a merry-go-round at a carnival, where smiling tykes, munching cotton candy, lobbied dad for *just one more ride—pleeeease!* It was more of an unsettling noisy on par with the shrieks echoing from inside the haunted-house ride.

Whether white, black, or Hispanic, our neighbors had this thing about hollering and screaming and slamming doors day and night. Perhaps taking a cue from their human counterparts, the constant blare of TVs battled it out at full volume. When evening rolled around, the banging of pots and pans signaled the neighbors cooking dinner. The pandemonium was further accented by crying babies, barking dogs, kids playing stickball, or someone picking a fight in the street.

On some nights, red emergency lights splashed bursts of hot color against my windowpane. The eerie light show involved hues of police blue or fiery yellow depending on the rescue service that had arrived.

## WELCOME TO THE JUNGLE

After the murder adjacent to our apartment, I wanted to spend as little time at home as possible. Getting some distance from the scene of the crime was therapeutic. You know, out of sight, out of mind. Playing outdoors with the neighbor kids quickly became a priority and, it turned out, I held the keys to unlocking new friendships: a baseball bat and ball. These tools of the trade were hard to come by in the neighborhood, making me an instant hit on the block.

After school we'd play baseball well into the evening. The apartment complex was your basic inner-city arrangement of two-story buildings facing each other with an asphalt courtyard in the middle. Naturally, we had to be careful where we hit the ball since we were surrounded by windows.

One day a grown-up wandered into our game. I had seen him before, but I didn't know his name. He wore faded blue jeans and ankle-high brown work boots. His well-tanned, muscular arms protruded from a black sleeveless T-shirt. Turned out, he was the dad of one of the kids, a construction worker by trade, evidently home early from the job site—or out of work. Didn't matter. We just liked having an adult getting involved with us.

I was at bat when, on the far side of the courtyard, the manager of the apartment complex strolled across the hot asphalt and announced his desire to get into the action too. He seemed sincere in his interest to join the game. He even had a mitt.

With two adults there'd be one for each team. Seemed to me like we were about to have our best game yet. Walking toward the makeshift pitcher's mound, the manager kept saying things like, "Here, kid, toss me the ball. I'd like to play with you guys. You know something? I'm a pretty good pitcher."

How was I to know that his real agenda was to take the ball away from us? As I'd discover later, the apartment manager didn't like kids playing ball in the quad and was determined to put an end to our sport. It didn't take but a second for the construction worker dad, who was more perceptive about such things, to figure out what was really going on. Like a volcano about to spew, he started getting worked up that the manager was trying to "rip us off" and that he'd "just have to teach him a lesson," only he used rapid-fire profanity to punctuate his growing rage.

Before I knew what was happening, this hothead erupted. He marched over to me, snatched the bat from my hands, turned, and headed toward the manager, wielding my Louisville Slugger as if it were a machete. I was horrified. I watched the bat swing through the air as the bully dad confronted the manager with a barrage of expletives.

*No way! He's not gonna hit the guy, is he?* I thought. I was an inner-city novice. I had spent second grade in small town USA. Yucca Valley was a quiet community where people never locked their doors. I was completely unprepared for the confrontation unfolding before my eyes. *Surely they wouldn't come to blows. What if the manager was carrying a gun? Would there be more yellow tape, more blood by the time this was over? Should I get help? Who would I ask, anyway? My mom and stepfather were both at work.*

*Now what? Should I run? Hide?*

*Pretend I didn't see?*

Paralyzed with fear, I froze at the plate.

There are some things no child should see. The sheer inhumanity of an outraged dad unleashing his anger on another human with a bat is certainly one of those things. And yet the six of us kids watched helplessly as the manager, unarmed, attempted to stave off the blow of wood against bone with just his mitt. Oblivious to the example he was setting, this father wailed away at the manager.

A moment later I heard, *Whack!* A dull thud echoed through the courtyard as the manager dropped to the ground, and doubled over, his head down between his legs. He grabbed his left wrist with the other hand. The blood dripped into a pool between his legs; his arm was badly broken with a compound fracture.

I ran. I *had* to get help.

I bolted to our apartment looking for one of my siblings, but nobody was home. I felt terrible. Responsible. Fearful. I mean, it was my idea to play baseball. Sure, I wasn't the one who belted the manager. I was just a kid. Still, I felt tremendous guilt for somehow causing his pain. I would have gladly stopped playing had I known what was going to happen.

With no one around to help and no one to talk to, I crashed on the couch and waited for my mom. I fought back a wave of tears.

When my mom finally got home, she was not happy with me. Not in the least. Boy, did she lay into me. After all, the "weapon" was *my* bat. I think she thought I had been doing something I knew was wrong, but I wasn't. How was I supposed to know we weren't supposed to play baseball between the buildings? Nevertheless, she insisted that I apologize to the manager. That evening, after the apartment manager returned from the hospital all bandaged up and with a cast on his arm, my mom ushered me to his unit and said, "I think you have something to say."

I couldn't take my eyes off of the blood soaking through his cast. To see this man in his late fifties nursing a busted arm because my bat was used to club him was almost too much for me. Between my racing heart and the fear churning in my gut, I'm not sure how I mustered the voice to offer an apology, but somehow, I did. To his credit, the manager was gracious and assured me it wasn't my fault. Looking back I'd say that God used this painful page in my life to model what grace looks like.

After that incident, my mom restricted me from going out to play for a very long time. That was the last time I played ball in Compton. In my view, none of this mayhem would have happened if Dad and Mom had just stayed together.

But they divorced three years before.

## FATHER KNOWS BEST?

My biological dad, Richard Daly, had been engaged in an ongoing affair with alcohol, gambling, and horse betting, but I'd say it was primarily the alcohol that lured him away from us. Something terrible must have driven him to find constant comfort from the bottle—the liquid mistress was too seductive for him to resist.

Despite many painful memories, I can recall delightful early childhood moments with him. Take Saturday mornings, my absolute favorite day of the week. I could smell sizzling bacon, freshly scrambled eggs, and toast even before I opened my eyes. The fragrance beckoned me out from under the covers to the kitchen where Dad hovered over the skillet. A dishtowel was always draped over his right shoulder as he worked his magic. I'd stand next to him as he arranged the steaming food on the plate with the flair of a seasoned chef. I loved being close to him. I felt safe by his side.

At 6'5", he was tall, fit, trim, and solid. I loved the way Dad would reach down, scoop me up in one arm while juggling the plate full of food in the other hand, and bring me to the table where the silverware and juice awaited. My dad worked for a furniture manufacturer, and so we always had great furniture in the house. I never wanted to leave his arms, but when breakfast called, I'd ease into my seat and turn my attention to the feast before me.

Still, there was a Dr. Jekyll and Mr. Hyde aspect to my father that I'd only learn about much later in life. I'm not talking about the drunken outbursts. Although rare, they were impossible to miss. Rather, I'm referring to his clandestine side, to the fact that my dad talked occasionally with my older siblings about being a runner for Chicago's most infamous gangster, Al Capone, as a boy.

If true, that would certainly explain a lot. My dad did grow up in Chicago and worked in the furniture business. Al Capone's business card described him as dealing in used furniture. Coincidence? Maybe. Stranger things have happened. Perhaps my dad's affinity for alcohol was an attempt to repress these memories.

Furthermore, if Dad had some connection to the kingpin of the Chicago crime syndicate, that could explain why my siblings and I don't know the first thing about our extended family. We had a mom and dad, of course, but that was the extent of our bonsai-sized family tree. As a kid, I never could figure out why we didn't have any aunts and uncles, or cousins, or grandparents like all of my friends. I still don't know.

Everything about my parents' past was shrouded in absolute secrecy. We didn't know anything about their backgrounds until years later, when, after their deaths, we discovered both Dad and Mom had three or four social security numbers. There's even a question about whether our real last name was "Daly."

Such a bizarre collection of details led us to believe my folks might have been in a government witness protection program. At least that would explain why they moved around so much during an era when most families stayed put in the same home for decades.

I remember listening to my dad share stories about his younger days playing baseball. He told fascinating tales of the year he played with the Detroit Tigers. I can't prove that he actually played ball with that team for two reasons: He's dead, which complicates asking any follow-up questions, and there's that lingering issue about our real last name. I have tried to sort out the fact from fiction, but so far I can't reconcile the stories. He *was* good at playing baseball, that much is true.

But did he really play ball at Tiger Stadium?

Or was it his drunken imagination?

My dad coached Little League for years and taught Mike and Dave how to play but, sadly, lost interest by the time I came around.

I wanted to believe my dad had made the major leagues. That would be a significant accomplishment on his part and would give me hope that I, too, might have the genetic stuff to play in the big leagues.

Or compete in the big time.

Or at least amount to more than someone who looked in the mirror every morning and doubted his future.

At the same time, it doesn't really matter whether or not Dad ever wore the Detroit Tigers jersey, batted .300, or managed to hit the winning home run. If he never threw a ball his entire life, he was still *my* dad. And I miss him. I wish he were still alive to go grab a cup of coffee, shoot the breeze, and help me find out more about my family tree.

## PROMISES, PROMISES

After my parents divorced, my mother was left with the Herculean task of raising five children as a single parent. We were living in a modest rented home in Alhambra on Fifth Street where the cockroaches were bigger than breakfast, lunch, or dinner. My mom worked two or three jobs just to put food on the table, and still there were days when we had nothing to eat.

When we didn't have milk, we'd mix Kool-Aid packs with water to pour over our cereal. Dad was pretty much out of the picture, except when he'd stop by the house to pick up a few groceries. Mind you, he didn't *bring* bags of food to feed his family; he came to *take* a few things for himself when he was down on his luck.

Once, when I stumbled on him taking food out the door, my appearance seemed to catch him off guard. He masked his surprise with a broad smile and then told me how much he loved and missed me. My reaction was somewhat guarded. *Dare I believe him?* His track record as the loving, caring father wasn't so hot—at least not of late. Sensing the distance between us, he told me he'd stop by later that day to bring me a baseball mitt for my seventh birthday.

A real, honest-to-goodness, genuine leather glove.

For me. From my dad.

This was the best news of the year. I smiled so hard, my face hurt. He tousled the hair on my head with a strong hand, turned, and then left me standing by the door, my heart hammering against my rib cage. When my best friend, Ricky, came over to hang out and play, I couldn't stop bragging. My dad was going to bring me a glove. A new leather baseball glove. Probably a Wilson special edition with a deep pocket for all of the balls I'd catch. It would be my first mitt.

Every fifteen minutes I'd run to the curb with Ricky to see if my dad was coming. We'd look down the street and study the landscape. Squinting, we saw no sign of him in the distance. Not yet. We'd go back in the house and play. Then, I'd announce, "I'm sure he's *got* to be coming now." Off we went, darting out the front screen door. Nope. No sign of him. This went on all afternoon. As the sun began to trade places with the moon, Ricky, who lived just a block away, headed home.

"Call me when he comes," Ricky offered with a friendly slug to my shoulder. Walking him to the curb, I managed a weak smile. I was only seven years old, but I wasn't entirely clueless. My dad had lied to me. At dinner, I picked at my food and asked to be excused early. My mom knew how disappointed I was. She tried to encourage me, but she couldn't replace my dad.

That night I retreated to the security of my bed. I clutched the corner of my covers and pulled them into a tight knot just under my chin. Hidden behind the soft folds of a thick blanket, I felt invincible. I was sure no under-the-bed or closet-lurking monster could get me as long as those protective covers were in place.

If only my covers could ward off the emotional blows dealt by my parents.

Alone in the darkness, I replayed the encounter with my dad in the kitchen—his smile, the roughness of his hand as he ran his fingers through my hair like a rake, the sound of his voice as he promised to return with a glove, and especially the warm feeling that came over me at the thought of his gift.

I tried in vain to silence the accusing voices in my head: *He never came. He said he was coming. He promised he would bring me my first mitt … but he never came.*

I pulled the covers around me tighter.

Would it be too foolish to hope that Dad would come in the morning? Chalk it up to childhood innocence, but part of me longed to find some plausible explanation for the no-show. *Maybe he got hung up in traffic. Could be that the store didn't have my size mitt, right? Or maybe he was having it gift wrapped?* At least those reasons were better than the alternative—that he never intended to keep his promise.

Dad never came.

I'd like to think that he had a perfectly good reason for failing to keep such a big promise to his seven-year-old son, but he didn't. My trust in him took a hard knock that day. I was no longer confident that he'd be there when I needed him.

Take something as simple as the issue of feeling safe and secure in the home, something that every kid ought to feel. It seems a dad ought to be the Defender of the Home. You know, the "go-to guy" when danger lurks in the neighborhood. The guy who locks up the house at night and makes sure we're safely tucked in bed. But my dad didn't even live under the same roof. Without the confidence that he'd be there for me, I lived in fear.

Especially after my clash with the Bully of Compton.

## JACK THE RIPPER

I wasn't the only white kid living in Compton, but I was certainly one of the few. For some reason Jack, another white kid in our complex, decided to make me his target. Jack was three years older than me and had the tough-guy attitude down pat. The guy both looked and acted like an angry fiend, from the military crew cut and dirty T-shirt to his snarly, blistered lips. He appeared to be perpetually frothing at the mouth, and for reasons unknown, Jack derived special pleasure in bullying me.

Perhaps if we were a little closer in age, I would have found the courage to confront him. He just seemed too big, too fast, and too much older than me. I didn't have any adults in my life that could handle the problem for me. My bio-dad was living who-knows-where, and even if he'd been around, past experience had taught me that I couldn't count on him. Certainly not in a pinch. My stepfather, while capable of defending the family, wasn't making any efforts to get close to me. I didn't feel comfortable telling him about Jack the Ripper.

Instead, I told my sister Kim.

"Kommander Kim" was one tough cookie. She knew how to

stand her ground and refused to take any flack. Kim didn't say a word after I told her about Jack, but I was confident she'd handle the situation in her way; in her time.

Not long after I confided in Kim, Jack was chasing me home from school. We both attended Starr King Elementary School, and since he lived around the corner from me, he'd routinely use that after-school trip home as an opportunity to show me what a tough guy he was. This time, I wanted nothing of it. I bolted as fast as my freckled legs could carry me. We came to the section of the apartment property where tall hedges lined one side of the sidewalk, forming a wall of thick foliage. With a busy street on one side and the hedge on the other, there was basically no escape for fifty yards. If I slowed down, Jack would be on top of me.

I glanced over my shoulder. Jack was right behind me, tracking me like a heat-seeking missile. A measly ten yards separated my face from his fist. With a burst of adrenaline, I managed to widen the distance between us. I sucked in gallons of air to cool my burning lungs. My shins were about to split. I tore past a slight break in the bush and saw something out of the corner of my eye. It dawned on me. My sister had come to the rescue.

Kim stepped through the hedge and popped him a good one. He never saw the punch coming. While he tried to find his legs, Kim towered over him and yelled, "Never mess with my little brother! Got that?" That was the last time I had to deal with Jack.

Kim is tough, tough as nails.

Frankly, it felt really good to have someone looking out for me. Normally, that person would have been my dad, but he wasn't in the picture. Keep in mind I'm not saying a man ought to use force to stop the taunts of a bully. Typically, a dad would talk to the bully's parents. I'll let you make your own mind up about that. However, I know I'd have taken great comfort if I could have gone to him and had the assurance that he was in my corner, that he'd go to bat for me in a heartbeat.

As an adult, I've had some space to process what went on with my father, both the good and the bad. I know that I cannot change the past by making excuses for his behavior or by whitewashing my history. He made a choice when he sent us that message in the bottle: He wouldn't be there for us, for me.

He wasn't there when I was terrorized by a bully.

He wasn't there when things got out of hand at a ball game.

And he wasn't there to teach me how to be a man, a husband, or a father who provides food, guidance, security, and love. The consequences of his choice not to get help for his struggle with alcoholism and, instead, to pursue his self-destructive ways, affected each of us Daly kids profoundly. There's something about a father wound that can really mess with you—for years, if not for a lifetime if you allow it … like the time Dad stopped by to deliver a message none of us could ever forget.

## 2

# If I Had a Hammer

My parents divorced when I was five. One of the more compelling memories from that difficult chapter of my life was a close encounter with a monster. Although my bedroom door was shut tight that night, I had no faith that its hollow panels would offer much resistance to that *thing* lurking on the other side. Lying alone in the dark, scared out of my wits, I did what I always did under the circumstances—I yanked the blankets over my little body and then pulled them tight to the base of my neck.

In those early years I had a thing for comforters—they represented a cloak of safety against the "momphers." At age four, while I couldn't properly pronounce "monster," I sure knew one when I saw one. At the moment, there was definitely a monster outside of my door.

This particular monster flopped into the brown corduroy reclining chair in our darkened living room as if he owned the place. A jug of Gallo burgundy wine sloshed and spilled onto his shirt as he took frequent swigs—right from the bottle. Armed with an oak-handled, ball-peen hammer, he sat with his right elbow draped over the edge of the chair. With repeated *thumps*, he struck the hammer slowly against the floor, biding his time. The tool probably weighed a full pound, but whatever its weight, it could inflict real harm.

I should know. The monster had already smashed a hole in our hallway drywall. This was no dream. I saw the whole thing with my very own eyes. My brothers and sisters and I were home alone. Mom was working at a nearby bowling alley. We were just hanging out in the living room, sitting on the rust-colored shag carpet popularized during the sixties. The walls had been painted a cross between hospital green and the color of pea soup, which gave the dimly lit space a sterile, muted feel. It wasn't much to look at, but it was our new home.

We were happily watching TV in our pajamas when the monster barged through the front door, unannounced. His forceful entrance sent the door sailing backward on its hinges and into the wall with a *wham!* His eyes were puffy, reddened, and glassy, and he searched the room with a fiery intensity that instantly spiked my internal alarm. His face, unshaven with several days' growth, appeared haggard. The words he mumbled were slurred as if his tongue were too thick.

I had to remember to breathe.

Up until that encounter, I'd never witnessed such a terrifying scene. As a typical four- almost five-year-old boy, I was intrigued with the mysteries and joys of life. Preoccupied with bugs, lizards, cars, toy guns, and the stuff picked from my nose, I had a healthy innocence that every child ought to enjoy throughout their childhood. But in an instant, my world was rocked forever.

I backed away toward the green sofa, instinctively aware that my forty-pound body was no match for this giant. The towering figure spewed a host of threats as he staggered deeper into the house in search of something—or *someone*. With a roar, the monster bellowed,

"This is what I'm going to do to your mother!" *Boom!* He swung the hammer with such force it bashed a giant hole in the wall. The house seemed to shutter from the blow.

My sisters started crying.

I would have cried too, if I hadn't been so terrified of drawing attention to myself. Plus, I was pretty sure monsters didn't like crybabies. Besides, I *knew* this man, or thought I did. He was a spitting image of my dad who had the same height, weight, build, and facial features as this crazed man. But this raving-mad drunk couldn't be my father.

So, the man stalking our house, while resembling my dad, wasn't the man I knew. To walk past him now, I fully believed *this* man might grab me by my hair and start wailing on my head just like he did the wall. He plopped down in the recliner and proceeded to drink from his jug with deep gulps.

Aside from the babbling TV and the occasional sniffling from my sisters, an uneasy silence settled on us. Now what? Even at age fourteen, my oldest brother, Mike, had this way of taking charge and keeping us younger kids out of harm's way. With the monster ensconced in the chair, Mike viewed this as an opportune time to hustle us into the back bedroom where he and thirteen-year-old Dave could put together a game plan.

Because Mike was the biggest brother, he decided to stay in the room with Dee Dee, Kim, and me to protect us while Dave, who could run like lightening, would slip out of the window and dash down to the bowling alley to tell mom. She'd know how to stop the nightmare.

At least that was the plan.

## ARRESTING DEVELOPMENT

For the better part of an hour, the muffled yet insistent tremor of steel against carpet pounded away at the frayed edges of my nerves. The hammer's cadence continued *thump ... thump ... thump ...* as the monster ticked off the minutes. The steady stream of thuds was as nerve-racking as the constant drip of a faucet, only much more ominous.

Even though Mike was doing his best to keep us calm, I knew my dad was still sitting in the living room in that reclining chair. I could hear the hammer strike the carpet through the bedroom wall. I closed my eyes as tight as I could, but it didn't help. If only I could plug my ears—or become invisible and slip out unnoticed.

*Where was Dave? Had he reached Mom yet? Was help on the way? What if Dad decided not to wait for her and, instead, targeted his rage against one of us? Would Mike really be able to stop him?* I didn't want my dad to hurt my mom. I didn't want my dad to be who he was at that moment.

I wanted my old dad back.

Was that even possible?

Dave was in full panic mode. Hysterical at the memory of what he'd just experienced, and motivated by the thought of what else might happen if he didn't hurry, he ran until his legs burned and begged for relief. There was no time to rest. He pushed harder, faster—the urgency of his mission propelled him on.

We had no choice but to wait for Dave to make contact. You might wonder why we didn't just call her on the phone. Keep in mind this was 1966, years before the invention of cell phones and personal pagers. Back then, rotary phones with their agonizingly slow and clunky dial were the standard mode of communication. Besides, unlike today's houses with phone jacks everywhere—even in the bathroom—our only phone was located in the living room ... precisely where my dad was seated.

Dave, covered in sweat and tears, bounded across the bowling alley parking lot, burst through the doors, and started screaming for my mom. Several bowlers closest to the front doors paused to observe the curious interruption. Dave scanned the room; there was no sign of her. The sound of dozens of bowling balls thundering across the wooden lanes continued. Dave yelled and then yelled some more. People turned from their games and shot him foul looks.

Dave ran to the counter, pushed past the paying customers, and demanded that the manager find his mother—*now!* She was *supposed* to be at work. She *said* she was at work. So she *had* to be at work. One problem.

Mom wasn't there.

His panic turned to desperation. Pleading with the manager, phone calls were made and, five minutes later, my mother strolled into the bowling lobby. Dave shouted, "Where have you been?" Mom told him not to worry, to calm down, and tell her what happened. "Calm down?" Dave barked. "Dad is going to kill you! He's at the house, he's drunk, he has a hammer, and he's gonna *kill you!*"

That got her attention.

She asked about the rest of us. Where were we? What were we doing? Were we safe? Dave fought to catch his breath. His words spilled out in a rush: "Mike's there doing what he can to protect the girls and Jim.... He's locked up with them in the bedroom.... I sneaked out the window.... We've got to get to them!" With that, Dave and my mom got into a friend's car and drove the short distance to our house. Rather than pull into the driveway, they parked on the street. Dave started to jump out of the car when Mom turned partially around in the front seat, made eye contact, and told him to stay put.

"Huh?" Dave said, his forehead wrinkled into a knot. "We've got to make sure the girls are okay. Let's go, Mom!"

"Honey, be patient," she said. "Let the police handle this." As soon as she spoke those words, two patrol cars rolled down the street, lights flashing. Evidently, her friend was an off-duty police officer who had called for the squad cars. The officers pulled into the driveway, parked, then stepped out of the cars with flashlights drawn. Sitting in the backseat, Dave watched as the police approached the house in the near total darkness.

"What will they do with Dad?" Dave wondered aloud, his nose pressed against the window.

"They'll get him some help," was about all she would say. To her credit, none of us ever heard our mother badmouth our father. Even in the days after their divorce, she refused to call him a drunk or a bum or in any way demean his reputation. Moments later, the police were escorting my dad to the police car. He pleaded, "Jan, this isn't necessary. We can work this out. Come on, Jan! Call off the dogs already."

Mom didn't say a word.

These events were taking place unbeknownst to me. I was still shaking under the covers. For all I knew, my dad was still sitting in the chair, waiting. Mike, Dee Dee, and Kim, however, heard what was happening and, after my dad was arrested, left me in the room to go and find Mom. With a click, Kim closed the door behind them— which really freaked me out. I think they were just trying to shield me from what was happening.

I pulled the lime-green blanket over my head.

It felt like an eternity before someone finally entered the room. I peaked over the edge of the covers as a policeman moved to the side of the bed. He rested his hand on my chest and said, "Son, are you okay?"

I managed a nod. "Sure."

He studied my face with a trained eye. He wasn't buying _ story. I sensed there was no harm in fessing up.

"Okay, so maybe I'm just a little scared."

A warm, knowing smile eased across his face. He said, "Trust me, everything will be just fine." With that, he turned and left ... and then closed the door. I hated the sound of the door closing. I didn't want to be left alone. I longed to jump into the arms of my mom. I needed to know that everything would be okay.

## HAPPY DAYS

Years would pass before I knew about the events that transformed my lovable dad during the first five years of my life into the lunatic bent on killing my mom in the "hammer house." To set the stage, I was born James Daniel Daly in July of 1961. I'm told my parents proudly brought me home from the West Covina Memorial Hospital to our home in Baldwin Park, California. Dad, it seems, viewed me as a special gift to them in their "old age;" he was fifty-one when I was born.

Our bungalow sat on a quiet dead-end street, largely sheltered from the unrest and commotion of life in the big city during the sixties. For the better part of four years, we had a "normal" family life. My brothers and sisters played baseball and rode bikes in the cul-de-sac. They had the time and freedom to make friends and explore the nearby woods. My mother stayed home to cook, clean, and be a mommy to her newborn child while my father held a steady job at U.S. Steel.

Best of all, both were sober.

In the years before my birth, things were downright ugly in the Daly household. Alcohol consumed my parents' every waking moment. One of my brother Dave's craziest early childhood memories was sitting in his booster seat at the kitchen table looking at a bottle of vodka in the middle of the table. Both of our parents were sitting next to him—completely passed out. They were so addicted to the bottle that they almost lost the right to raise my brothers and sisters.

I also learned there was a pattern of drunken fights predating my arrival. My oldest brother, Mike, said our parents constantly fought over stuff that he didn't understand. Even as a four-year-old, Mike saw the effects of what was going on around him and started to believe that their arguments were somehow *his* fault. Mom would say something provocative; Dad would swear and shout something nasty back. She'd throw a pan or whatever was within reach. Before long, the cops would come knocking.

Mike recalls one serious clash where Dad was beating up on Mom. When the police arrived, they put my brothers and sisters in the back of the police cruiser to take them to the Los Angeles County Children's Home. Mike was four; Dave, three; Kim, two; and Dee Dee, just one. While sitting together in the cop car, the overhead beams of red light served as a beacon alerting the neighbors of their embarrassing exile. In time, the police appeared at the front door of the house ushering my parents outside—wrapped in blankets.

Evidently, they were both too drunk to get dressed.

Dave recalls how they were removed from my parents' custody that night and taken to a children's shelter. He was directed to a bed in the back corner of a large, open dorm-style room. As he and Mike were escorted into the dorm, he wondered, *What are all these beds doing here? What am I doing here? Are we being punished for something? Where are Mom and Dad?* After a bath and something to eat, my siblings were put to bed with a head full of unanswered questions. My sisters were separated from their brothers and sent to a different wing of the same facility.

By the time Mike was in second grade, my siblings were sent to either a children's home or placed into foster care on at least four occasions. Although Mom would stop by for a number of supervised visits, they were not together as a family.

Somewhere along the way, my mom managed to snap out of her drunken stupor. During one of the visits at a foster-care facility, Mom announced, "Kids, I promise you'll never have to go through this again."

The fact that my folks struggled with alcohol was not a surprise. They first met at an Alcoholics Anonymous meeting in Chicago; they were just two broken people working to set aside their pasts and hoping to create new memories together for the future. Nothing like a fresh start and new beginnings, right? They had their first son, Mike, right off the bat. Mom was thirty-four and Dad was forty-two. Not long afterward they moved from the Windy City to New Orleans, where Dave was born, eighteen months after Mike's arrival.

Once again, they picked up and moved, this time to the Mile High City, Denver, where Kim was born. For reasons that aren't clear, they didn't linger in Denver, but headed to Los Angeles where Dee Dee and then, years later, I was born. While all of this relocating may seem normal by today's standards, at the time most people never moved beyond fifty or so miles from their hometown. They lived thirty or forty years in the same house with the same phone number and, for the most part, held the same jobs.

Why, then, did my parents move us around?

What compelled them to keep from putting down roots?

What's more, a close inspection of our birth certificates reveal a variety of different last names given by our parents. For example, my birth certificate listed my last name as "Daly" while my older brother Mike's birth certificate gave him a different last name. Adding to the mystery, my mother used three different last names between the five of us children. Clearly, there was some dark cloud hanging over them that would be important enough to keep changing addresses, names, and social security numbers. As I mentioned before, this pattern of change could have had something to do with my dad's prior involvement as a runner for Al Capone. It's possible they were in the government witness protection program. We just don't know.

What is clear is the fact that the most difficult demon to shake was their habit of reaching for another drink, which is why, when my mother promised my siblings that they'd never have to live in foster care again, she was dead serious. There would be no U-turns. No more benders. No more late-night brawls leading to arrests. Those days were over.

Someway, somehow, she dug down into the core of her being and found the inner strength to break the cycle of addiction, brokenness, and parental irresponsibility she had exhibited for so long. She wasn't particularly a "religious" person; there wasn't a "come to Jesus" moment at this stage of her life. She just *knew* things had to change—*would* change—because she didn't want to lose all that was dear to her.

I believe her change of heart is an early picture of God at work in my mom's life. Even though she didn't necessarily know where her strength to change was coming from, God was at work behind the scenes. He knew how her story would ultimately unfold—just as God knows how ours will unfold—and graciously provided her with the courage to make a stand.

Once Mom made the commitment to get sober and begin caring for her children, she laid out the options for my dad: He could join her in laying off the bottle and raise the kids as responsible parents, or, he should just clear out and let her take care of things. Again, to his credit, my dad wanted to take the high road.

He wanted to be there for Mike, Dave, Dee Dee, and Kim. Which is why, when I came on the scene, I didn't even know what "drunk" was. In what I see as a gift from God, throughout what child development experts call the ever-important "formative years," I only experienced the best that my dad had to offer. Every time I walked past my dad, he'd reach down and scruff up my hair with a playful sign of affection. I sensed that I was special to him. Sometimes he'd wrestle or toss me into bed with a tickle. And while he rarely hugged me, I felt very much loved and completely safe in his presence.

With that issue settled between them, Dad and Mom regained custody of the children, and moved to Blackwood Street in Los Angeles for a brief stint before finally settling on Cosby Street in West Covina. As it turned out, their move to Cosby Street was a divine arrangement. On the day that they moved in, the couple who lived next door introduced themselves as Bud and Esther Hope. The connection was an instant hit. They became not only best friends with my parents, but our adopted grandparents.

Grandpa and Grandma Hope. What great names.

More than that, it was a fitting name for the role the Hopes ultimately played in our lives. (That part of the story comes later.) Suffice it to say, life on Cosby Street produced the sweetest experiences for my siblings, and I have delightful memories of my early childhood there. Mom and Dad were finally settled, sober, and happy. The Hopes were great friends, and by all appearances we had a "functional" family.

However, that Kodak moment in our history would change in a flash.

## BAD COMPANY

Four years after moving to Cosby Street, temptation for my dad came knocking in the form of a friend from work, Joe Garcia. Joe visited several times over the Christmas break bringing his version of the holiday spirit—a fifth of whiskey. The enticement of hard liquor and the peer pressure to imbibe were too strong for my father to resist. He caved, and then caved again. In a short period of time, Dad started drinking regularly although he did a fantastic job of hiding it from me.

As a recovering alcoholic, however, Mom knew the telltale signs of his addiction and promptly reminded him of the terms of their commitment. When there didn't appear to be any serious change in his choices, she announced, "Richard, if you're going to continue this, I'm going to leave you." Of course, I didn't know anything was particularly wrong between them. My older siblings didn't comprehend the full scope of my mother's concern either.

The drinking continued.

And she left.

Mom hastily packed our bags and took us away from the only home I'd known. She timed our exodus to coincide with the time Dad would be at work. What's more, she had no intention of informing Dad of our new digs, which, as you might guess, ultimately infuriated him. When Mom told us we were moving, we were confused. Why wasn't she telling Dad? Was this some sort of new game? A grown-up version of hide-and-seek?

Mom said get packed, so we packed.

Mom said, "Don't tell your dad," so we didn't.

We moved into one of the many nondescript, single-story white stucco duplexes on Heines Street in Los Angeles, California. Two memories linger from our brief stay at that address.

First, our front yard was a battlefield of sorts: Patches of grass fought a constant encroachment by the dry earth. The dirt won most days. Occasionally, the grass would create an unholy alliance with the weeds for supremacy of the yard. We didn't live there long enough to aid the lawn in its cause. The second recollection involved the monster and the hammer. There was no way we could live within those walls after what transpired. The memories were too fresh, too painful, too savage.

The entire wretched episode might have been avoided, or at least postponed, if not for a freak encounter between my sister Dee Dee and Dad. Several weeks after we had moved away from Cosby Street, Dee Dee was riding her bike when, quite by accident, she saw Dad walking toward her in the distance. Their eyes locked for a brief second, and, with Mom's admonishment echoing in her mind not to tell Dad where we lived, she turned around and peddled for all she was worth.

She could have gotten away clean since Dad was on foot and she had wheels. They were several blocks away from our house and she had a solid start. However, when Dee Dee reached our house, she threw her bike on the front yard, darted in the front door, and announced, "Mom … *Mom!* I saw Dad. He was coming down the street."

Dad had been searching the adjacent neighborhoods to Cosby Street looking for any sign of us. He'd been patrolling the streets for weeks. Now, spying Dee Dee's bike in our front yard, he made a mental note of our new location and then left to do two things: find a hammer to drive home his point, and get tanked up on Gallo wine to steel his nerves.

In many ways, that night was a watershed moment. Like a gravestone, it marked the death of my parents' marriage. We would never again be a family. From then on my dad became a figure that would breeze in and out of our lives—candidly, he was more *out* than *in*. I lost a lot on that sleepless night—we all did. Our identity as the Dalys would be diluted in the shuffle of temporary relationships and living arrangements that spanned more than twenty houses.

Gone, too, was the serenity and the stability of the family life we had enjoyed. Personally speaking, the most significant loss was my belief in the man I once looked up to with immeasurable admiration. Before the hammer incident, my dad could do no wrong. But with each swing of the hammer, he drove home the conviction that I would never want to grow up and be like him.

# 3

# Mother Knows Best

I should be insane—or in jail.

At least that's what folks often say when they hear the details of my story. The fact that I've managed to avoid those outcomes has much to do with the kind of resilient woman my mother was in the face of hardship. Without Dad's regular paycheck and presence in the home, life took a turn for the worse. While Mom worked hard to make the most of what we had, little did we know how difficult things would become.

In a few short years, I'd lose my mom to cancer and become an orphan. Thankfully, the kind of home environment she worked to maintain, one that balanced discipline with an extra dose of laughter, prepared us to face the future with optimism.

My mom was tall—about 5'10"—slim, and in good shape. She had dark features—olive skin, black hair, and hazel-brown eyes. She was half American Indian and half Irish, with the Indian side the more dominate. Her tenacity probably came from the Indian side; her playful wit and humor from her Irish ancestry.

With Dad now out of the house, my mom was thrust into life as a single parent of five—long before single parenting had a network of resources and day-care services tailored to their unique needs. Without a dad to anchor the home, we were all headed into uncharted waters—the murky details of that voyage will surface in future chapters. For now, let me confess I'm afraid I didn't make things easy on Mom.

When I was born, according to my sister Kim, I was irresistibly cute. Make that "the cutest baby that's ever been born." A real happy baby, too. Always smiling. No all-night crying fits. Kim remembers the afternoon I was carried home from the hospital. Mom carefully laid me down on my parents' bed. Kim wasted no time climbing up for a closer inspection. Moments later she announced, "We've got a live dolly!" Eyes filled with wonderment, she remembers deciding right then and there that she'd be a mommy one day too.

By age six my angel wings had fallen off. I became very much the spoiled brat and could do no wrong, at least in the eyes of my mother. I was rarely punished, primarily because my older brothers and sisters would cover for me. I'm not sure why. They probably wanted to keep the peace since they knew from firsthand experience just how bent out of shape my parents could get. This pattern of covert cover-up continued long after Dad and Mom had gone their separate ways.

I remember exhibiting one of those "Picasso Moments" that children are so fond of having. I stumbled upon a tube of my sister's bright red nail polish and decided it was the perfect medium in which to express my budding creativity. Using the television screen as my canvas, I got busy.

Within seconds I had painted the red pigment all over the glassy surface with the unbridled flair of an impressionist artist. Stepping back to admire my handiwork, I heard my sisters Dee Dee and Kim enter the living room. I can't say that they shared my enthusiasm for the final product. More accurately, they flipped out.

"James Daniel Daly! What have you done?"

With a shrug, I feigned innocence.

Hand outstretched, Kim motioned for me to hand over the bottle. "That's *my* nail polish. Give it here."

I flashed a dopey grin as if to say, "Nail polish? What nail polish?" But I was busted, and I knew it.

Dee Dee chimed in. "Boy, Mom is gonna be *so* mad."

Instinctively, my sisters took it upon themselves to clean up the mess before my mom could see the damage. Dee Dee dashed out of the room; when she returned, she was armed with nail polish remover and a roll of paper towels. Together, Dee Dee and Kim scrubbed away all evidence of my infraction. Just about the time they had finished cleaning, a new thought crossed their minds:

*Jim won't get punished if the evidence is erased.*

They weren't being vindictive: Kim and Dee Dee just decided that I had been pampered and coddled long enough, and they were going to do something about it. Sure, life was hard, but it was time for me to grow up and face the consequences of my poor behavior. Retrieving the remains of the nail polish, they quickly rescrawled broad strokes across the TV screen.

Here's the funny part: I never did get into trouble. I'm not sure why. Maybe my mother was too tired to make an issue of it. And, technically speaking, I didn't paint what my mom saw when she came home from work. Ironically, my sisters were now out of nail polish remover, and for days we had to watch TV through the prism of red blotches. Perhaps it was mom's way of allowing all of us to share in the consequences of our actions.

While grateful that I had escaped punishment, my footloose, spoiled-brat days were numbered. Clearly, my sisters had gone over to the Dark Side and could no longer be counted on to run interference for me. And, I could sense that my mom knew something had to change. As it turned out, it took one well-placed punch to knock some sense into my young, insolent noggin.

## KARATE-CHOPPING MOM

I'm pretty sure one reason Mom let me slide was because of the regrets she had. She felt incredible guilt that I no longer had a father in my life, and I believe she did what many parents are tempted to do in that situation: She overcompensated by giving me everything I wanted. Every time we'd go shopping, I'd get a toy. Being a typical six-year-old in the late sixties, I was captivated by all things G.I. Joe. I stocked up on G.I. Joe action figures, G.I. Joe clothing, G.I. Joe jeeps, G.I. Joe *everything*. I scored tons of Hot Wheels gear, too. Miles of orange Hot Wheel tracks. All of the coolest cars.

No toy was out of bounds for me.

And not just toys—chocolate shakes, too.

Now that Dad was not providing financially for us, Mom had to juggle two and three jobs at the same time. Her long hours away from home only served to further amplify the burden she felt. To compensate, she'd often bring home a chocolate shake and place it in the fridge so that it would be there in the morning for me. While a semi-melted shake might sound gross, it separated in such a great way: The rich, yummy cream sat on the top and the chocolate milk rested on the bottom.

I loved it.

If she'd forgotten to replenish my shake stash, I'd run out to the car in the morning as she backed out of the driveway to remind her. I'd grab on to the car door in my pajamas and plead, "Are you going to bring me a chocolate shake tonight? You forgot last night." Usually she would say, "Yes" or, "I'll try." Sometimes she'd actually say, "No," and I could tell it pained her to disappoint me.

But the grocery store was my ace in the hole.

I tagged along with my mom whenever she went grocery shopping because I *always* got a toy. If I didn't get one, I'd rant and rave and throw a full-body tantrum—the kind of fit that turned the heads of other moms who, with their pious looks, questioned what kind of mother would deprive Junior of such a simple request. Rather than put her foot down, she'd give in and allow me to run over to the toy section to pick something—*anything*—that would silence the whining.

My typical modus operandi was to start working on her from the backseat of the car. I planted the first thought in her mind by wondering out loud what G.I. Joe outfits might be waiting for me. We'd park, grab a shopping cart, and head through the sliding glass door. That's when I'd turn up the heat and make a bigger deal about picking out my toy. After all, there was usually an audience within earshot. I could play to the crowd with the best of the spoiled brats.

However, like most kids at that age, I had this profound fear of getting lost in the store, of not being connected to my mom. For reasons not fully understood by me at the time, my dad was no longer around. At times, an emptiness welled up in me, and I'd wander through our home totally missing him. Naturally, the last thing I wanted to do was lose my mom at the grocery store. So, on one hand I had this fear of letting Mom out of my view, even for an instant. On the other hand, I was determined to get my toy.

These conflicting feelings of fears and desire played tug-of-war in my head one Saturday afternoon when Mom and I headed to Crawford's Grocery Store in Alhambra, California, to do the weekly food shopping. As we made our way to the produce section, Mom

45

stopped by the fresh corn display where I knew she'd take her time carefully sorting through the husks in search of the best-looking ears. I announced, "Mom, I'm going to go get my toy, okay?"

It was more of a pronouncement than a sincere request for permission. Getting a toy, after all, was my inalienable right. Without waiting for her consent, I quickly added, "Are you going to be right here when I get back?" She nodded, although I could tell she was distracted. I had clearly lost my audience to the science of selecting yellow corn. "Go ahead, Jimmy, I'll be right here," she said.

"You *promise?*"

"Yes. Now, run along. I'll be here."

Even at age six I knew exactly where the toy aisle was. That land of make-believe awaited just beyond the mountains of toilet paper, plates, and assorted paper goods a few aisles away. With my radar set on autopilot, I hustled over to find the G.I. Joe camouflage outfit I had seen on a previous trip. I didn't buy the camo gear then since I had my heart set on a different "must have" matching accessory. Due to my one-toy quota, I had to wait.

Wanting to make sure I got the garment before they ran out of stock, I sped to the shelf. Standing on my toes, I plucked it from the rack and then gawked briefly at the prize now in hand. Happy with the latest addition to my collection, I headed back to Mom. The whole trek to Toyland only took about three minutes.

That's when I saw my mom four or five aisles removed from the produce department—walking *away* from me. I blinked. There was no mistake. She was standing next to the cans of soup. I knew it was her because she was wearing her black polyester slacks (that's back when polyester was in vogue), black blouse with brown paisley swirls, and flat-heeled dress shoes. Her hair was tucked and pinned in the back.

*What's this?* I thought. *Mom said she'd be waiting for me ... by the corn. Where does she think she's going without me?* I panicked. The fear of abandonment and the anger I felt that she hadn't kept her promise to be where she said she'd be sent me reeling. With the energy of a charging beast on opening day of the annual run with the bulls, I tucked my head down and ran directly toward the bull's-eye on her back.

With the target almost within reach, I clenched my fist into a tight ball and raised it over my head hatchetlike. I came down on her hard. Clobbered her was more like it—right between the shoulder blades. I didn't know I was capable of such a powerful swing. I actually heard a thud as my fist hit her square in the back.

G.I. Joe would have been impressed.

The sudden and full fury of my fist completely knocked the wind out of her. With a forced exhale, she groaned and staggered a half-step forward. She instinctively groped for the nearest shelf in an attempt to recover her balance.

Still hot with anger, I stared upward at the spot on Mom's back where I'd just whopped her as if daring her to turn and face my wrath. I was prepared to unleash a barrage of indignant words. *How dare you leave me! You promised you'd be over there, not here. What kind of mom doesn't keep her promises?* But the words never left my tongue. With a slow, guarded motion, my mom turned around to make sense of what had hit her.

As she rotated full circle, the puzzlement in her eyes was only matched by the bewilderment that I felt. It was my turn to stagger backward several short steps. My heart spiked and my legs went wobbly as the earth beneath me caved in.

*She wasn't my mother.*

The woman whom I had just decked wore the identical top, pants, and shoes as my mom. The pale skin on her face, pulled taut as a drum, wasn't anything like the soft, warm features of my mother's face. Her eyes zeroed in on me like lasers.

"What *are* you doing?"

"I ... I ... I thought you were my mom."

That freaked her out.

Before she could say another word, I backed up and darted out of there. Somehow through the flood of tears soaking my face, I found my mother—exactly where she said she would be, still shucking the corn. Evidently, my sobbing caught her attention. Mom turned, lowered the husk, and said, "What's wrong, Jimmy?"

"I just hit a woman."

"You *what?*"

"I just hit a woman."

"Why in the world ..."

"... because I thought it was you."

Her right eyebrow shot up indicating that I needed to offer a little clarification, especially since I had never hit my mom before. I tried to articulate my fears. *I thought she had left ... because she wasn't here but there ... although she was really here, but I didn't know it at the time.* I don't know whether or not my explanation made much sense. My mom's reaction, however, was crystal clear. She put down the corn, suddenly all business, and said, "Jimmy, you need to go back and apologize to her."

I balked.

Her tone revealed that there wasn't room for negotiation, I had to apologize, end of story. With her arm resting on my shoulder, she quietly escorted me to the scene of the crime. Apologizing all by myself was a frightening prospect. I started praying for a miracle ... if only the lady had left the store, even on a stretcher, just as long as I didn't have to face her again. No such luck. She was still stationed midway down the aisle.

Standing next to the end cap display and just out of view of the other woman, Mom waved me forward. I froze. I felt as though my legs were bogged down in freshly poured cement. Chipping away at my reluctance, my feet managed to slowly move forward. I shuffled past the soup, feeling less like the animated G.I. Joe action figure of a few minutes earlier. As I approached, I could see her face was still tight with anger. She put a hand on her hip and waited.

I offered a sheepish, "I'm sorry that I hit you."

She looked down at me with no attempt to mask her indignation. "Why did you hit me?"

"I thought you were my mother."

I looked down at my feet just to be free of her glare. An uncomfortable moment passed. I glanced upward and added, "I'm sorry."

She shook her head, the corner of her mouth twisted up in disgust, and then turned away. I turned away too, happy to get out of there.

That experience had a profound impact on me on several levels. I never, ever hit anyone again. Choosing to use my fists to resolve conflict began and ended that day.

I also discovered that my mom's word was golden, that when I failed to control my anger, I blew it big-time, and that making things right and admitting your mistakes is all a part of life.

To her credit my mom never rubbed my face in my behavior. I didn't feel judged. She wasn't trying to shame me in front of the woman in order to preserve her own image. There'd be no "Excuse my dumb kid" lines offered on my behalf. She just wanted me to take responsibility for my actions.

The other thing I so appreciate about my mother is the way she did her best to make our house a place of fun and laughter. She knew we kids needed both guidance *and* a generous serving of lighthearted giddiness. Which most likely explains why she arranged for me to meet Larry of the Three Stooges.

## NYUK! NYUK! NYUK!

At age seven, I was a member of the Three Stooges Fan Club. More of an honorary member since I never actually mailed in a postcard to join. As a quasi-member in good standing, I watched Moe, Larry, and Curly often, parroting their eye poking, face slapping, and finger snaps with my siblings. I stopped short of taking the frying pan to the coconut of my brother Dave.

There were actually six different Stooges during the span of that hit TV series. Moe Horowitz and his real-life brothers Shemp and Curly were all members of the trio during various stages of their slap-happy careers. They, along with Larry Fine, Curly Joe, and Joe DeRita rounded out the popular act. Hands down, Curly was my favorite. He seemed to catch the brunt of Moe's teasing and yet always managed to keep a smile on his face.

I haven't watched all 213 episodes, but one of my favorites was "Disorder in the Court." At one point the judge summons Curly to the stand and then attempts to place him under oath. Part of that bit still sticks in my mind:

> JUDGE: Do you swear …
> CURLY: No, but I know all the *woids!*

My mom, knowing how much I loved their antics and how I'd rehearse a few of their lines, called me one morning with a special treat in mind. She was waitressing at the Big Sky Country Club in Yucca Valley, California. My mother had this winsome way of making friends. Never shy where strangers were concerned, she befriended many of the regulars. Which is why this particular morning she asked if I'd like to meet Larry from the Three Stooges.

Clutching the phone to my ear, I couldn't believe what I was hearing. "Meet Larry? *Soitenly!*"

Mom laughed and told me to get ready; she'd pick me up around 11:00 a.m. Talk about pure excitement. This was the "poifect gift." What kid wouldn't want to have lunch with Larry? I floated to my bedroom and looked for something to wear that wasn't too dorky. This was, after all, *Larry*. The last thing I wanted to do was to come across like some kind of a knucklehead. I rummaged through my box of clothes. Satisfied with my selections, I got dressed and then waited anxiously by the front door like a puppy desperate to go for a walk.

Twenty minutes later Mom and I were walking through the expansive halls of the country club. I'd never seen such luxurious surroundings in my entire life. My feet seemed to sink into the plush green and black floral carpet. Massive white columns reached from floor to ceiling like California redwoods. We entered the dining room and strolled past tables draped in white linen tablecloths, bedecked with some pretty snazzy-looking silverware, cups, and plates.

My heart was thumping so hard I wasn't sure my chest could contain it. I wondered if Larry would look like he did on TV. You know, would he have the same Athenian-style bushel haircut with the bald spot in the middle? Would he wave his hand in my face and try to poke out my eyes while adding a "woop woop woop" sound effect?

Suddenly, I wasn't sure what to say … or what to call him. My mom always taught us to speak respectfully to adults. Saying, "Hi, Larry!" was definitely out. I wondered whether "Hi, Mr. Stooge" would be appropriate, but quickly ruled that out too. I could almost hear Larry saying, "Mr. Stooge? Don't be an imbecile."

I looked up at my mom and reached for her hand. She was wearing a black skirt and white blouse with a black pocket belt to hold her change, order pad, and other waitressy necessities. She seemed so confident. As if reading my mind, she said, "Jimmy, relax and just be yourself. This will be great!" She must have felt my sweaty palms and known I needed her reassurance.

After passing through the general dining room, we turned left at the bar and entered a semi-private eating area. Several four-top tables had been pulled together to make one longer table. A simple floral centerpiece was placed on each setting. Padded high-back chairs with bear-claw feet were situated around the table. About seven people were sitting with Larry.

Sure enough, Larry had his haircut like the Greeks of old. He wore beige pants and a white dress shirt with a T-shirt visible through his open collar. A brown leather jacket was draped over the back of his chair. Larry sat facing the window overlooking the manicured golf course. I wasn't sure if he'd ever played golf. I knew Larry played the violin professionally and was once into boxing as a lightweight fighter, but somehow the whole picture in front of me felt a little squirrelly.

I mean, to my way of thinking, the Three Stooges were ill-mannered mavericks. They threw pies in people's faces. They didn't eat pie from china and discuss how to improve their golf game. With TV shows like "Malice in the Palace" and "Pies and Guys," both with their legendary pie fight finales running through my head, it was just a little bit odd to see Larry dining in this context. Still, it was great to be standing in the presence of a real live television star.

My mom pulled a chair up for me at the end of the table right off of Larry's left elbow and motioned for me to take a seat. Taking her place on the other side, she introduced me to Larry. Larry finished chewing a bite of his sandwich, looked over at me, and said, "Hey, kid … doing all right?"

I found my voice. "Yeah, doing great."

After that rather weak introduction, I sat there staring like a dog expecting a treat. He continued to eat and talk with his other guests, tossing me an occasional smile. Several minutes passed. No face slaps. No eye pokes. The whole time I thought, *Now what? Is that it? This guy isn't even funny.*

I shifted in my seat starting to feel awkward about the visit. Larry was trying to carry on a conversation with seven adults while I wanted him to do some of his Three Stooges shtick. Ten, maybe fifteen minutes later, Mom excused us. She took me to another table in the general dining area and brought me soup and a grilled cheese sandwich. With a broad smile, she asked if it was fun to meet Larry. I told her, yeah, it was fun to meet him—because on some level it really was. None of my friends could say that they'd met a real Stooge.

What's more, my mom was doing the best she could to create a fun memory. I'm convinced that her efforts to put fun in our home went a long way in keeping us sane and on the right side of the law. She also showed us how to use humor when we were hurting or disappointed. She had this playful way of easing the pain—like taking out her teeth, messing up her hair, and placing her thick-rimmed glasses upside down on her nose. How could we keep a sad face when she did that routine?

Unfortunately, a few short years after meeting Larry, Mom fell ill with a cancer that would take her life. No amount of humor could compensate for the loss I felt, but I'm getting ahead of the story. Just before she died, I encountered one of the biggest, toughest, and angriest members of the human race.

# Hank the Tank

I entered the military when I was eight years old.

I had no say in the matter. In fact, I was enrolled against my will. Completely unprepared for this sudden turn of events, my whole universe changed overnight. One day I was a happy kid in the third grade at Bixby Elementary School, and suddenly I had to endure a regiment of push-ups and other strictly enforced maneuvers designed to break my will and transform me into a good little soldier.

Appealing the decision to enlist was not an option.

My drill sergeant was a big guy, probably 6'3" and 205 pounds of muscle. He looked a lot like Telly Savalas who played Kojak on TV, only my sergeant's ears were bigger. His head was completely shaven. He wore no glasses, chains, or rings. Unlike other military types, he didn't have any tattoos, either. He didn't need them. He had the solid build of a Ukrainian or a Viking.

But that nose—I'll never forget his overhung nose. He had this crook in his nose that reminded me of a vulture. Of course, I could never say that to his face, that is, not if I wanted to live another day.

I entered boot camp in 1969.

That's the year my mom married Hank Sheldon. There was no

church ceremony with friends to witness the event. There were no flowers, photos, or fancy embossed invitations. There wasn't a reception. Mom showed up one day at the house and announced she and Hank had gotten married in Las Vegas. None of us kids had known she was even going to Vegas.

Then again, Hank had a pilot's license and so it was entirely possible for them to fly down for the afternoon, tie the knot, and fly back all in the same day. One thing was certain. When Mom married Hank, it rocked my world in a big way. Hank, you see, was ex-navy who apparently forgot the "ex" part of the deal. The day that our new stepfather moved in with us was the day that my stint in the military started. He viewed our house as his personal barracks and my siblings and me as his little platoon.

From day one Hank made it clear he was the commander of the ship and we were to fall into compliance—or swab the deck. He immediately waged an aggressive war on dust, dirt, fingerprints, and unfolded blankets. The guy was a neat freak on steroids. With the flair of a real fanatic, he'd check under our mattresses for stuff. He'd open kitchen cupboards and drawers and require the girls to wipe out any dust lurking behind the plates, forks, and spoons. Windows and windowsills had to be spotless.

Good enough was never good enough.

Hank ran the house like a drill sergeant. Worse, he had a militaristic … no, make that a *sadistic* discipline technique. He would make me hang up my jacket fifty times because I'd left it on the floor in my bedroom, or fold my blanket a hundred times because it was crumpled on the bed. Let me just say that this approach to enforcing the rules was a bit foreign to us.

Which is why I nicknamed him: "Hank the Tank."

Equally fed up with his control issues, my sister Kim risked a serious backlash by writing this anonymous note:

*"Our house is clean enough to be healthy*
*… and dirty enough to be happy."*

When Hank saw the note taped to his bedroom door, he went nuts. He demanded to know who the author was. None of us stepped forward. That only further enraged him. Hank didn't like to be crossed. Ever. Hank had come from a wealthy family. He was disinherited because he decided to join the navy against the wishes of his parents. Even then it was his way or the highway. If joining the navy meant he'd be cut out of his parents' will, so be it. He wouldn't be held hostage by such threats. Crossing this man was never a good idea.

For the better part of thirty years, Hank served in the navy. Although a real tough guy, he opted to become a chef on the side. Every port of call, he'd go ashore and learn some new aspect of cooking. Hank became a real whiz with a knife and spatula. After he left the navy, he worked as the head chef at the Glen Restaurant, an upscale eatery not far from our house. That's where he met my mom, who had taken a job there as a waitress.

Frankly, I'm not sure what she saw in the man.

To us, Hank was nothing but trouble. His love for Mom, though, was unmatched, I'll give him that much. He adored her. He doted on her. His fondness for her was unmistakable. You could see it in the way he looked at her, spoke about her, and acted around her. But Hank's love for us was missing in action. We were nothing more than excess baggage. He resented the fact that he had to share Mom with us. He'd been a bachelor his entire life and was unaccustomed to dealing with kids—the five of us were way more than he'd bargained for.

The conflict with Hank was constant and borderline legendary. He had no idea how to relate to my teenage sisters. He didn't know how to meet the needs of a nine-year-old boy. About the only person he made any connection with other than Mom was my brother Dave, primarily because Dave helped him in the kitchen. Even so, Dave had to watch his step ... or face the wrath of one knife-throwing chef.

## THE IRON CHEF

When Hank walked into a kitchen, he became god of the grill. He put the "iron" in iron chef. Hank wanted things done his way or his temper would ignite like a red-hot blaze. My brother Dave, who was seventeen at the time, knew this from personal experience.

The first summer Hank was a part of our family, he got a contract to provide the food service for the Mammoth Mountain Inn in central California. That was no small deal. Mammoth Inn was a world-class ski resort, perched nine thousand feet above sea level on the eastern slopes of the Sierra Nevada Mountain Range. Nestled against the mountainside, the inn had breathtaking views from its sweeping plate-glass windows. During the summer, the ski business was exchanged for groups of hikers and assorted outdoor enthusiasts. Dave tagged along as Hank's "assistant" and was assigned to be the prep guy.

Hank also hired a local kid to be the dishwasher. According to Dave, the dishwasher was always kissing up to Hank, trying hard to make points. Dave knew better than to play that game with Hank the Tank and warned the guy to back off. No matter how many times Dave would tell the dishwasher to "stay away from Hank," the advice fell upon deaf ears.

One morning, Dave and Hank arrived in the kitchen to prepare breakfast for about 150 hikers. Try as they might, they couldn't find the omelet pans. These weren't ordinary omelet pans, mind you. These were Hank's personal pans—his pride and joy. They had served him well for years. When he couldn't locate his trusty cookware, Hank started to flip out. As any craftsman will tell you, you don't mess with a man's tools.

Having searched every inch of the place, Dave decided to check inside the giant, industrial-size dishwasher unit. Sure enough, he found the four omelet pans sandwiched inside. The kid they'd hired ruined Hank's prized pans by running them through the machine. Dave held them up and blurted, "Hank, I found them. They were in the dishwasher!"

Hank went ballistic. For the next five minutes, Dave watched as Hank launched into a salty tirade peppered with a heavy dose of spicy language: "An omelet pan is *never* to be washed … water is *never* to touch them—ever! They are conditioned with steel wool and vegetable oil … what kind of *idiot* doesn't know that?" Dave got a crash course that day in what it meant to curse like a sailor.

Midway through the meltdown, Dave watched the clueless dishwasher walk into the kitchen through the back door and then stop midstep. With a dopey grin on his face, he said, "Oh, I see you found my surprise!" Hank was beside himself. He grabbed a butcher knife and threw the blade at the culprit. With a pinging sound, the blade slammed into the wall and lodged about two feet from the startled kid. Dave shot him a look as if to say, "I told you not to mess with the Iron Chef."

That was the last time they saw the kid.

For the next eight hours, Hank made Dave take steel wool and a gallon of vegetable oil to recondition the four pans. Periodically, Dave would stop and hand a pan to Hank who, in turn, placed it on the fire. Taking an egg, Hank cracked it into the pan. After several moments of swishing it around the reworked surface, Hank would announce, "Nope. It's not ready. Wipe it out some more."

Hank's perfectionism and unbridled temper were destined to cause a major division in our home. While I was too young to do anything but follow his orders, my siblings started to mount a mutiny of sorts. My brother Mike, who, at nineteen, was serving in the navy, was the first to fire back. Mike, who freely admits he was somewhat of a hothead back then, came home on shore leave once and heard how Hank was treating us. He wasted no time in reading Hank the riot act.

Standing toe-to-toe, Mike jabbed a finger in Hank's chest and said, "I'll tell you two things. If you ever hurt my mom, or make her unhappy, or if you ever hurt one of the kids, you'll have to deal with me. Got it?" It was like watching two bucks sparring for dominance of the pack. From then on, whenever Mike was scheduled to come home, Hank disappeared until Mike left.

Don't get me wrong. Hank wasn't all bad news. In fact, there was one routine that he introduced into the family that was a good thing: He insisted that we start praying before meals. Hank wasn't a Christian, per se. He had more of a mushy religiosity somewhere in his background. I can't say that he owned a Bible. I never saw him reading from one and he most certainly never read it to us. He just had this belief that we ought to fold our hands and give thanks before a meal because "that's just what we're supposed to do."

The idea of praying resonated with me. I liked the thought that we were talking to God. Looking back, this practice of "saying grace" was another unexpected gift from God. He knew a day was approaching when I would become aware of my need to rely upon Him. These nightly dinnertime prayers, such as they were, paved the way for a much more meaningful conversation with God down the road. They were also further evidence that God was at work behind the scenes. I'm grateful that Hank took the lead in this area.

In spite of this worthy contribution, Hank was a constant source of tension. For her part, my sister Kim had had enough and refused to yield to Hank's overbearing ways. The friction was so great she ended up running away from home for several months. The tipping point was an altercation over a Frisbee, my Frisbee. We were playing catch in the backyard when I accidentally threw the Frisbee through a window on the garage. Hank barreled through the back door and barked, "Who broke the window?"

I had two choices.

I could lie—and avoid a few hundred push-ups.

Or, I could tell the truth and face the consequences.

Thanks to my mom's guidance, I had learned the importance of owning my stuff back in Crawford's Grocery Store. I opted for the truth. I started to say, "I did it," but before I could get the words out, Kommander Kim snapped. She kicked into high gear and braced for a fight.

Kim said, "I did, *Hank*. So, what are you gonna do about it?" She added a sprinkling of her own sailor lingo to underscore her point. Everything about her stance screamed, "BACK OFF." While they didn't come to blows, Hank yelled back and chased Kim around the family car in the backyard like a rottweiler. She bolted down the driveway and down the street. After successfully evading the madman, she packed what little she had and moved out.

I couldn't believe my eyes.

Just like that, Kim was gone. I was watching my world unravel right in front of me, and was powerless to prevent it from coming fully apart at the seams. My dad was gone. My brother Mike was off in the navy and rarely home. Now my sister Kim had left, leaving me stuck under the thumb of Hank the Tank. While I still had Dave,

Dee Dee, and Mom, I was completely blindsided by what was in store for us just around the corner.

## FROM BAD TO REALLY BAD

I never saw the death of my mother coming.

All I knew was that she started to become tired most of the time. Exhausted was more like it. Without warning, this energetic, fun-loving, and hardworking woman—who used to bring me chocolate shakes and make us laugh—quit her job and spent her days isolated in her room. Although I couldn't help but notice the radical change in Mom's behavior, I just thought she was sick. Sick people needed to rest. Sure, she looked a little pale to me. She had lost a few pounds, too, but I just figured that went along with being ill.

How was I to know she would be dead in a few months?

Her true condition had been kept from me. My mom had been diagnosed with colon cancer and had undergone a colostomy—a surgical procedure to insert an external excretory bag. I'd only learn about that years later. At the time, however, I was preoccupied with a puzzle: Why weren't we permitted to be with her? Had we done something wrong? Did we cause her sickness? Was her illness contagious? Nothing made sense. She was my mom and we should be together, that's all there was to it.

The answers to my questions boiled down to one word:

Hank.

Mom was in lockdown because Hank had ordered it. He was so obsessed with her that he wanted her all to himself and worked overtime to keep us from seeing her. He thought we tired her out.

Sometimes she would wander out of her bedroom to sit on the sofa and talk with us in the living room. The minute Hank came home, he'd lower the boom. Right in the middle of the conversation he'd interrupt and say, "Jan, come here, you need your rest." Like a prison guard, he'd take her arm and lead her back into solitary confinement.

That really bothered me. I hated to have her taken from me. Why couldn't we be together? My mother had cared for us through both good and hard times. Why wasn't I permitted to do the same for her when she was sick? Okay, maybe a nine-year-old wasn't capable of giving her medical care, but at least I could have *talked* with her, right? I'll never understand why Hank didn't let me give my mom a hug or a kiss before she was ushered away. With a click, the door would close behind them and I'd be left on the outside longing to be by her side.

About this time, Kim returned home and couldn't believe that Hank was preventing us from seeing Mom. On several occasions Kim picked the lock on the door in order to get in and sit with her. During one of those visits, Kim asked Mom why Hank kept us locked out. Evidently, Hank claimed he was afraid one of my older siblings would steal her morphine shots for their own use. I don't think they were into drugs, so I'm not sure where Hank got that idea.

Clearly, Hank didn't know how to deal with death. He didn't attempt to explain what was going on with Mom's health. He didn't think to prepare us for the inevitable. He lacked the courage to wade into those waters. Like a storm brewing off in the horizon, this strong, rock-solid navy man knew what was coming and was beginning to crack under the pressure. His way of coping and maintaining order was to separate us. He also started hitting the bottle pretty hard toward the end of my mother's life. The thought of losing her was killing him.

As the end approached, Hank's behavior changed. He still made incredible meals. After all, cooking was his outlet. I remember he'd first take Mom, who was locked up in the bedroom, something to eat. When he returned to the kitchen, we'd sit down to dinner and, as became our habit, he'd say, "Well, let's pray."

Only now, instead of rattling off one of his formula prayers, his voice would catch. His emotions bubbled up under his fortresslike exterior and began to surface. He loved my mom, deeply. But just as soon as the feelings surfaced, he'd stuff them back down, clear his throat, and carry on.

Since I had been kept in the dark and didn't know Mom was dying, I just figured Hank was really, really sad that she was sick. Looking back now, I'm pretty sure the reality of her impending passing overwhelmed him. Especially the thought that he'd have to take care of kids whom he didn't love and with whom he had no real connection. He must have thought, *Dying and leaving me with five kids wasn't part of the deal, Jan.*

Dave remembers a particular Sunday when Hank charged into his bedroom and, with a shake, woke him up and said, "Dave, come on, we're gonna go to church." Mind you, our church affiliation at this time was nonexistent. Since Hank didn't know which church to attend, the two of them drove around looking for the biggest church they could find. Perhaps he thought that the bigger the church and the higher the steeple, the closer they were to God. Of course, that's not how it works.

They ended up at an Episcopal church with large stained-glass windows and heavy wooden pews that appeared to have been hewn by the Pilgrims. Massive brass organ pipes covered the walls behind the pulpit. The thick red carpet, which covered the narthex floor by the front doors, rolled down the main aisle and then up three short steps to the altar. The sanctuary wasn't particularly full. They entered and sat toward the rear.

As the choir sang, Hank's emotional dam breached; tears of grief flowed freely. Dave had never witnessed Hank showing any real, unbridled emotion whatsoever and was at a loss for what to do. He wasn't about to put an arm around the man. They didn't have that kind of relationship. Dave wasn't even sure if he should look in Hank's direction for fear of getting hammered by a hymnal. Tough guys didn't like people staring when they cried. Dave played it safe and just focused on the dimly lit surroundings.

Hank buried his face in his hands and continued to fall apart. As the service ended, Dave decided he had better get some help. Walking to the front, he set his sights on finding the priest with the biggest, fanciest robe. Dave approached the older gentleman and said, "Please, you've got to come talk to my stepfather." When the priest asked what was wrong, Dave said, "I'm pretty sure my mom is dying and I don't think he knows how to handle it." He gladly obliged. While Dave sat out of earshot, the priest spent thirty minutes talking to Hank.

On the drive home, Hank stared straight ahead and didn't say a word. He could have shared the insights and comfort spoken by the priest. I'm sure Dave would have appreciated that. At the least, he could have used those private moments to probe Dave's feelings. This was, after all, Dave's mother who was dying. Oblivious to the needs of the seventeen-year-old young man riding next to him, Hank remained quiet.

Evidently, his pride as a self-made man got the better of him in the days ahead, too. He acted as if the whole close encounter with God on that Sunday morning never happened. While Hank was a closed book, my mom took a different approach with me. She never mentioned that she was about to die, and yet she creatively planted in me a remarkable picture about life, death, and new beginnings that I'll carry with me the rest of my life.

## FLOWERS FROM HEAVEN

For my ninth birthday, Mom surprised me with the ultimate gift. No, not another G.I. Joe toy. I was pretty much through with that stage. She got me a bicycle. Not just any regular old kid's bike. This was a blue Stingray with racing tires and an extra-large sissy bar—a tall, U-shaped chrome bar rising six feet into the air from the back of my sparkling metallic-blue banana seat.

I went everywhere on that thing. I was the King of the Road.

One particular afternoon, I arrived home from school and noticed my mother's bedroom door was both unlocked and ajar. I knew Hank would be hacked, but since nobody was around, I figured it might be safe to venture in. When she heard me hesitating by the door, she called out.

"Jimmy?"

"Yes, Mom?"

"I'm glad that's you. Come here, Son."

Happy to finally be in her presence, I covered the ground between us quickly and stood next to the edge of her bed. I really wanted to climb up and hug her, but she seemed surprisingly frail. There was so much I wanted to say. I mean, this visit was one of the precious few times that I got to see her in several months.

As my eyes adjusted to the soft, indirect lighting, I noticed her reddish brown, shoulder-length hair had been cropped short. She was much thinner now, of that I was pretty sure. She appeared somewhat smaller, as if her peach nightgown was a few sizes too large. She rested on her left side, a pillow propped against the headboard for support. It was difficult to believe that this was the same lady, with that great sense of humor, who dressed up as an infant by wearing a giant diaper to a party just for laughs.

With a weak yet beautiful smile, Mom explained her request.

She asked me to go to the nearby department store, which had a nursery, and buy a packet of chrysanthemum seeds. She wanted me to plant them outside of her bedroom window in the flowerbed.

Chrysanthemums?

Never one to miss a teachable moment, she told me to get a pen and paper. I zoomed out of the room, grabbed the items from a kitchen drawer, and then hustled back as fast as I could. I had to return before Hank came along and locked me out. After all, I was about to be sent on an important mission and didn't want Hank to sandbag it.

Mom slowly spelled out "chrysanthemum" and made sure I had written it down correctly. She pressed some money into my hand and, with a love tap, sent me on my way. I, of course, was happy for the chance to do anything for her. This was a big deal. She had singled me out from the rest of the kids. The fact that she trusted me with such a big assignment was like a gust of wind at my back. I rocketed toward the store.

Of course, I had never planted anything in my life. I didn't know seeds from weeds. But, if Mom thought I was up to the challenge, then I just had to get this right. The last thing I wanted to do was to fail her. Upon my return, I read and then reread the instructions on the back of the seed packet. I wanted to be precise with my gardening. If the directions called for three seeds per hole, planted every four inches apart, then that's what I'd do.

With ruler in hand, and garden hose ready, I planted a dozen chrysanthemum clusters in the flowerbed just outside of her window. It was a perfectly straight row, too. I measured those coordinates twice before pushing my forefinger down to the appropriate depth. I think even Hank, the perfectionist, would have approved of the job I was doing.

In an odd way, I felt connected to my mom as I worked. This

was our project. We were a team. She had the idea and I got to make it happen. I kept thinking, *Boy, she's gonna really love 'em ... and won't she be surprised when they bloom just like the picture on the packet.*

With a steady hand, I counted out the precise number of seeds, dropped them lovingly into each hole, and, with a gentle pat so as not to crush the life out of them, painstakingly refilled the holes. I served the thirsty seeds their first splash of water. That was the only time I remembered to water them. Gardening was not a priority for a nine-year-old, especially one with a blue Stingray and roads to conquer.

Thankfully, I planted in mid-February, when California was entering the rainy season. Mom's chrysanthemums would get the moisture they needed. After cleaning up, I went inside to tell Mom that the job was done. She was asleep, breathing slow and steady in the darkness. I retreated from her room, careful not to wake her. As it turned out, that would be the last time I was permitted to be with my mom at home until the very end.

## THANK YOU, MOM

Several weeks later, Mom was transferred to the hospital. As far as I was concerned, she was still just really sick. Mike, Dave, Dee Dee, and Kim knew better. Mom's health was failing fast. She had very little time left. Maybe days. Perhaps a week. Hank knew this, too, and went off on a bender. His drinking spree took him out of the picture for days. The man fell completely apart. Without any adult to turn to for direction, my siblings went into group mode.

After a family meeting, they were convinced that I should see Mom at least one more time. One problem. Back then, children under sixteen weren't allowed to see patients. My siblings staged a covert operation to smuggle me into the hospital on Saturday morning. It went off without a hitch.

We stood in a semi-circle around her bed. A thin, light-brown blanket lay loosely over her body. She sat in a semi-upright position with the bedrails in place. A translucent tube ran from the back of her left hand to an IV drip. But what struck me most about our brief visit wasn't the array of monitors with their constant beeps, or the hospital with its disinfectant smell.

My most striking memory is how my mom was so uplifting and positive. In spite of the pain she must have felt as the cancer worked overtime to shut down her vital organs, she joked with us. She laughed with us. She teased us. And her smile made each of us feel like everything would be "okay." Mom was giving us a gift—our last memory of her is one of laughter, of joy, and of love.

As we were leaving, Mom pulled Mike aside and said, "Look, I just want you to take the kids somewhere. I want you to go and have a good time, you know, get away from here. Maybe go up to the desert or the mountains and see friends."

Mike hesitated. "Shouldn't I be here with you?"

She persisted. "Will you just do it—for me?"

He agreed. This was what she wanted and he wasn't about to argue. With the exception of Dave, who decided to stay at our house, we left the hospital and headed east of Los Angeles. I'm not sure how we knew about this family out in the boondocks, but Mike was sure that we could hang out with them. Midway through our afternoon visit, Mike announced that he wanted to call Mom and see how she was doing. But, I learned later, he didn't want to call from the house because in his heart he had this sense that she had died.

Instead, he drove to the nearest pay phone and placed the call. He asked to speak with Jan Daly—or was it Jan Sheldon? The nurse asked him to hold. The minutes dragged on. Mike was starting to become anxious. The tight quarters of the phone booth didn't help matters. At 6'5", he was, after all, a big guy. He shifted in the cramped space and continued to wait. Was his premonition right?

The nurse came back on the line and announced, "You'll have to call the doctor."

Mike said, "Wait a minute, I don't need to talk to the doctor. I'm her *son*. I'd like to talk to my mom."

"I'm sorry," she said, maintaining a practiced professional demeanor. "You'll need to speak with the doctor."

"Fine. Then put him on."

"He's not here."

Mike was ready to reach through the phone and grab her by the collar. "So why don't *you* tell me what's going on? I was just with her this morning."

"I can't tell you. The doctor has to tell you."

A wave of fear washed over him. *Tell me what?* Mike cleared his throat and said, "Look, get the doctor ... get any doctor on the phone. I just want to talk to my mother." That's when reality hit him full force. He swallowed hard, and when he found his voice, said, "She's dead, isn't she? She died; that's why I can't talk to her, right?"

The nurse wouldn't budge. "You have to talk to the doctor."

Mike slammed the phone down. In his anger, he busted the telephone booth. Stumbling out, he fell down into the sand, crying. With fists clenched and repeated pounds to the earth, he wailed, "*This isn't right.... This isn't right.... There's no reason for Mom to die. This can't be happening. Not now.*"

Mike stood, kicked the sand, and got back in his car. He knew he had to compose himself during the short drive back to the home we were visiting. One by one, he called Dee Dee, then Kim, and then me into the kitchen to break the bad news. I remember Dee Dee coming out, first, crying. I thought, *This isn't good.* When Kim appeared, she was crying too. I thought, *Nope, not good at all.*

When my turn came, Mike said, "I don't know how to tell you this, Jimmy, but I think Mommy has died." Even though I wasn't sure what it meant to "die," I knew it had to be really bad. I mean, Dee Dee and Kim were bawling away in the other room. Suddenly, I realized that I'd never see her again. I fought back the tears. I could feel the edges of my ears start to burn and an emptiness settling into the place where my heart once was.

I reached for Mike's arm and squeezed—hard. Mike tells me I squeezed with such force I left deep nail marks. It's as if by holding on to Mike's forearm, I was somehow refusing to let go of my mother … if I could only hold on, maybe she'd still be with us. I think by clamping down I was recognizing the ache I felt inside. Dad was gone. Hank was off somewhere disconnected from our pain.

Now, Mom was gone.

One by one, the adults in my life had vanished.

And yet, over the next few chaotic days, Grandma and Grandpa Hope would deliver some of the greatest news I could ever receive.

# 5

# Home Alone

I stood beside my mother's graveside sporting my best corduroy pants, white shirt, and blue clip-on tie—the kind nine-year-olds wear on important occasions. I might have looked sharp, but inside my jumbled emotions had my stomach in knots. When my fourth-grade classmates at Bixby Elementary had heard the news, they sent me a batch of fifty cards, including several from the teachers. They said how sorry they were to hear about my mom. Some promised they'd pray for me.

The graveside service was about to begin. Though I was in a crowd of well-wishers, I longed for space. If another well-meaning stranger pinched my cheek and asked, "Are you okay, Jimmy?" (according to the word on the street, I still hadn't cried), I'd probably have gone nuts. Couldn't a kid be allowed to process his feelings in his own way? And what's with the pinched cheek?

United in their sadness at Mom's passing, hundreds of people I'd never met, and didn't know, had followed us from the funeral home to the cemetery. While these people had been Mom's friends, I felt overwhelmed by the crowd and definitely on the outside of the group. Everyone was older than me. I don't recall seeing one kid standing with us among the sea of gravestones.

I concluded this was not a place for children.

Maybe the death of my mother was just a bad dream, a nightmare from which I'd soon awaken. I looked upward. Had it really been just five days since Mom died at Long Beach Memorial Hospital? I searched the sky for answers that didn't come.

A thick blanket of cottony-looking clouds hovered overhead, cloaking the afternoon sky behind a shroud of gray. Unlike thin, wispy cirrus clouds on a sunny day, this array hung low across the horizon, obscuring the sun. I watched as unseen currents of air shuffled and reshuffled the gray-bottomed clouds, as well as the pages of the minister's Bible.

The pastor started to speak, pulling me back to earth. He offered words of assurance and read from the Bible. Much of what was said didn't register with me. My mind was elsewhere and nowhere at the same time. It's as if I had pulled an invisible blanket over me—as I had done many times before in bed with my covers—to shield me from the fear of the unknown. This time I needed to keep the ghostly feelings of abandonment from haunting me. I felt terribly alone. I desperately wanted to be held by my mother.

*Why did she have to leave me?*

*Where was she now?*

*People said she was in heaven, but where was that?*

My mind drifted like a kite without a string. I floated back to a memory from the funeral service earlier that afternoon. The chapel had been filled to overflowing, with maybe five hundred in attendance. People were lined up around the outer wall and spilled out of the back door. Since we didn't have any extended family, these people were all her friends.

After all, Mom was quite the extrovert. She'd walk up to a complete stranger if she wanted to meet them and say, "Tell me about yourself."

Position meant nothing to her. In her view, you were a person no different from herself. If she wanted to talk to you, she did. That's how she met and befriended all three of the Three Stooges at the Pomona Fairgrounds. No wonder the chapel service had been packed.

I recall how a tall, somber man in a black suit had directed each of us to the casket, one at a time, to place a rose and say our final good-byes. Mike went first. Then Dave, Dee Dee, and Kim. I went last. I don't know why they always made me go last. I was always out of the loop; the last to learn about how sick Mom really was ... the last to know she had died ... and now, the last to say good-bye.

When my turn came, I walked toward the open casket feeling the eyes of everyone in the chapel boring a hole into my back. I kept telling myself, *I've gotta be grown up. Don't cry. Just don't cry.* The pressure of being studied by a room full of strangers was enough to terrify me. And the thought of kissing my mom good-bye, which Kim had suggested, was not sitting well with me. I didn't think Kim would go forward with it, but she did. She leaned into the coffin and actually kissed Mom before placing a rose in there.

As I made my way down the aisle, I debated whether or not I could, in fact, bring myself to kiss Mom. Moments later, I found myself peering over the casket, numbed by the whole surreal experience. Being a few months shy of my tenth birthday, I was tall enough to be chest high with the top of the elevated coffin. My mom lay slightly below my eye level. She appeared pale and gray and definitely not "her." I tipped up on the balls of my feet to lean in closer.

I whispered, "Mom? It's me ..."

Boy, did I struggle to fight back the tears when I realized she'd never answer, couldn't answer. She was really gone. Slowly, tentatively, I reached forward and touched her hands. That was a real shock. Her fingers felt fake, like cold wax. They didn't feel anything like the hands that used to scratch my back. Mom would sometimes cup my face in the palms of her hands and look me in the eye to tell me she loved me; those hands were soft and warm—nothing like these stony limbs, which were more suited for a mannequin.

For a long moment I froze, trying to process the sight of my mom lying lifeless in the casket. The casket was an ornate bronze, watertight model we kids had picked out since Hank was too distraught to coach us into making a wise decision. Nobody told us it was just a coffin. We spent far more than we could afford. At least Hank had the foresight to purchase two plots at Roosevelt Memorial Park, one for each of them.

Looking at her porcelainlike face, I couldn't bring myself to kiss her. Instead, I told her that I loved her and placed my rose with the others. I turned and, refusing to cry, faced the packed room. I didn't want them to think I was just an emotional kid. I had so many unanswered questions running through my head. *What was death? Where was Mom now? Could she see me? Hear me? Was this really the end?*

*Would I see her again?*

That day changed me; at nine years old I became an adult out of necessity. I didn't know if my biological father was dead or alive, or where he was living. He had been a no-show at the funeral, just like Hank. Both of the men in my life were AWOL. We later found out that my dad didn't learn about Mom's death for several months after the funeral. And, for his part, Hank was back on the bottle, an old habit that resurfaced with all the pressure caving in.

We were on our own. Walking away from the casket, I started to feel stress about issues children shouldn't worry about. My mom's passing affected my survival. *Where would we live? What would we eat? What school would we go to? Who would pay the bills and take care of us? Hank? Was Hank capable of taking care of us? Would I even want him to?*

It's funny how your mind works in moments like that. While wrestling with adult-sized questions, there were also practical, little-kid things that tugged at my heart. I was sad that Mom wouldn't make me breakfast anymore. There'd be no more chicken and dumplings with scalloped potatoes and spinach on Sundays, a tradition and one of my favorite meals. My tenth birthday party was just four months away and mom wouldn't be throwing me a party.

I collapsed into the seat next to my siblings in time to overhear my sisters fuming. They were steamed about the way Mom was "presented." They didn't like her hair, her makeup, and they absolutely detested her outfit—the lime-green chiffon dress looked "ridiculous." Personally, I was too lost in my own fog of emotions to have formed an opinion one way or the other. I remember thinking: *Does it really matter?*

## STAIRWAY TO HEAVEN

With a host of thoughts weighing on my heart, I looked over at the minister. His voice sounded strained as he fought to be heard without a microphone. The brisk March wind didn't help matters. Pointing skyward with Bible in hand, he declared, "Friends, Jan is in a better place. For the Scriptures tell us, 'To be absent from the body is to be present with the Lord....'"

While I liked the sound of that, I wasn't exactly sure how it worked. I mean, I was pretty sure her body was in the box suspended over the giant hole in the ground several feet from us. How, then, could she be in heaven at the same time? At the time we weren't religious. Heaven, hell, and the afterlife were vague concepts. In matters of faith, we were, at best, CEOs—Christmas and Easter Only churchgoers.

Of course, like true CEOs, we never went to the same church twice. We might attend a Baptist church on Christmas and a Catholic parish for Easter. The next year we'd go to a Presbyterian church for Christmas and a Methodist for Easter. The churches with the kneeling pads were my favorite. I thought the pads were footrests. I often felt like lying down on them, but Mom would have frowned on that.

You can imagine, then, how my ears perked up when Grandma and Grandpa Hope stopped by with some unusual news earlier that week. Their visit came a couple of days after Mom had died. We were at home talking about the funeral arrangements. Actually, I wasn't doing any of the talking. Those were issues for my siblings to work out. The Hopes were kind to visit, and I was comforted to see them again.

You may recall the Hopes were our neighbors on Cosby Street— back during the happy days of my childhood. Dad and Mom became their best friends, and we kids quickly "adopted" the Hopes as grandparents. They, in turn, loved us as if we were their grandkids. When the Hopes learned Mom was dying, they had paid her a visit in the hospital.

Sitting on the sofa, Grandpa Hope conveyed the story. Over the weekend their daughter, Penny—we affectionately called her "Aunt Penny"—had asked, "Is Jan saved?" Unsure about Mom's faith in God, Grandpa said, "I don't know. Let's go find out." Off they went. Aunt Penny, and Grandma and Grandpa Hope took up positions around Mom's hospital bed. I could picture the room as he narrated the story.

According to Grandpa, he had taken her hand and said, "Jan, you know how much we love you. Because of that love, we want to make sure you're going to go to heaven. Do you believe that Jesus died for your sins? Have you invited him into your heart to be your savior?"

As he spoke, Grandpa's questions for my mom had taken me by surprise. While I had never given such matters much thought, I always assumed Mom would get into heaven because she was a "good person." She did her best to teach us right from wrong. She even taught us the Golden Rule—to treat others the way we wanted to be treated. That had to count for something, right? Plus, she made it clear that lying and cheating were out of bounds. Now, by the sound of it, those things weren't good enough to get her into heaven.

Mom must have felt something was missing in her life. Come to think of it, she'd been struggling with spiritual issues for some time. About six months before her death, Mom placed me in a weekly "release time" program at a local church. Every Wednesday afternoon, I was dismissed early from public school and "released" to go study the Bible at a nearby church for an hour. She wanted to make sure her "little guy" would get some kind of spiritual training and religious instruction.

And, she admitted to Grandpa that she couldn't say for *sure* whether or not she had a place in heaven. With the question of her spiritual destiny unresolved, Grandpa had asked, "Would you like to settle that issue right now?"

A smile eased across her face; "I'd love to!"

They joined hands around her bed as Mom prayed and gave her heart to God. Fourteen hours later, Mom stepped out of her frail, cancer-ridden body and into the arms of the One who awaited her in eternity. Grandma and Grandpa Hope had the honor of sharing that life-changing moment with her—and couldn't wait to tell us.

While I didn't understand the full implication of Grandpa's story, at least not until later in life, his confidence that Mom was in heaven comforted me. It sure sounded like good news. I liked the idea that she felt no more pain. I had this sense that God would take good care of her. I still didn't understand how her body was *here* and she was *there*. Maybe I'd grasp it one day, I thought. With the memory of Grandpa's visit and the story he shared fresh in my mind, I looked skyward again.

*Was Mom in heaven right now looking down on me?*

*Did she know how much I missed her?*

Lost in those reflections, I half heard the minister asking us to bow our heads for a final petition before he dismissed us. As he began to pray, I confess I hesitated to close my eyes. Frankly, I couldn't stop staring at the swirling clouds. They began to drift away with remarkable speed. Like a curtain pulled back from a window, the gray veil above was giving way to the deep blue skies beyond. I was captivated.

By the time the minister said, "Amen," a remarkable thing had happened. Most of the clouds had dissipated. Sprays of warm sunlight hurried to trade places with the shadows, like some sort of time-lapse film shot in the plains of Montana. We were now immersed in the golden glow of a late-afternoon sun. A handful of large cotton ball-shaped clouds lingered. Considering that the other clouds had jetted off to parts unknown, these lone stragglers stood out.

As the minister prayed, the wind continued to blow, causing the remaining clouds to morph gracefully into the definite likeness of a staircase, leading from cemetery to heaven. By the end of the prayer, the wind had finished its sculpture. Everyone was looking up now.

The image was unmistakable. The five of us Daly kids who, as nominal churchgoers, didn't look for symbolism in the skies, witnessed the sight. The Hopes saw it too. People to our left and right were elbowing each other, discreetly pointing toward the stairway to heaven.

Was it some sort of a sign?

Perhaps a message from Mom?

## LEAVING ON A JET PLANE

Mike, Dave, Dee Dee, Kim, and I piled back into the longest car in the world, at least that's what it seemed to me. Some sort of black stretch Cadillac DeVille, or maybe a Lincoln Continental, with charcoal-tinted windows. As the lead car in the slow-moving processional, we snaked our way through a maze of granite tombstones. Here and there I saw monuments with bouquets of flowers resting in their shadows. Several elaborate headstones towered over adjacent plots, as if boasting, "My gravestone is bigger than your gravestone."

While the staircase in the sky had scattered, I turned my head and, with a squint out of the rear window, briefly focused on where the flight of stairs had first appeared. In my mind's eye, I pictured those heaven-bound stepping-stones and wrestled with what they might have meant—if they meant anything at all. Minutes later, the limo pulled past the entrance gate, aided by a policeman who halted the oncoming traffic. The manicured, parklike cemetery faded from view as we merged into the congestion of Los Angeles traffic.

It felt strange to leave Mom behind.

I rode in relative silence. It would be a short trip to the McCormick Gardena Chapel where our car was parked, and I didn't feel like talking. Someone suggested we grab dinner on the way home, but I wasn't hungry. More than anything, I was drained. I was plagued by far too many fears and misgivings that, like a swarm of gnats, wouldn't go away. I couldn't help but wonder: *What horrible thing would happen next?*

After picking up our car at the chapel, Mike drove us home. The sun was beginning its nightly descent; its warm orange rays glinted across the windshield. I felt chilled. I couldn't shake the uneasy feeling that something horrible was around the corner. Minutes later, Mike pulled into the driveway. I was glad to be finally home and far away from the cheek-pinchers. Heading for the house, I was anxious just to spend time in my room, away from any commotion.

I stepped through the front door and gasped. I felt as though I'd been sucker-punched. I stopped dead in my tracks, gawking at the sight before me. Nothing made sense. I was exhausted, but I wasn't dreaming.

I blurted out, "Guys, where's all of our stuff?"

While everything had looked normal on the outside of the house when we arrived, the living room was completely vacant. The television was gone. The lime-green sofa was gone. The pictures, the books, the vacuum—everything had vanished. Mike, Dave, Dee Dee, and Kim pushed past me and quickly fanned out to the other rooms. The reports were shouted like a series of blasts from a rapid-fire gun.

*Empty. Empty. Empty. Empty in here, too.*

The beds, the chairs, the dishes, the towels, the refrigerator, and every lick of furniture—the house was completely empty. Well, almost empty. Our clothes and a handful of personal possessions had been tossed from the dressers and dumped on the floor in jumbled heaps. This was not a good sign. A week ago, Hank would have punished us with a hundred push-ups for piling our things on the floor.

Did someone forget to pay the rent?

Were we being evicted?

Had we been robbed?

We gathered in the now barren living room to consider our options. That's when Hank appeared from his bedroom carrying two suitcases. Mike was livid. Kicking into battle mode, Mike said, "Just where do you think you're going? What happened to the furniture and our things?" Hank waved him off. Usually quick to respond with a verbal jab, Hank didn't say a word. There was no fight left in him. Brushing past Mike, he headed out the front door and to the curb.

His shoulders slumped as if pulled down by the weight of the earth's gravity. No spark remained in his eyes. He had mentally checked out months ago. Hank the Tank was a broken man. We meant nothing to him when Mom was alive—and apparently less now that she had died. We followed him in the near darkness to the sidewalk, with the sun already below the horizon. When Hank finally spoke, the once confident bulldog shook his head and said, "I can't deal with this. I'm moving back to San Francisco."

He didn't say, "I'm sorry about your mom," or, "I hate to leave you guys this way," or, "Here are the arrangements I made for you guys after I'm gone." Nothing.

Mike was itching to get in his face, but probably knew a confrontation would accomplish nothing. Almost on cue, a taxi pulled to the curb. The driver helped Hank toss his bags in the trunk. They climbed in and headed for the airport. Like a phantom, Hank had appeared and then evaporated before our eyes. I never saw or talked to him again.

Back inside, we stood around the empty living room talking about how Hank just left. The fact that he was an emotional wreck was clear. I can't say we were that surprised he chose to abandon us on the evening of Mom's funeral. And, at least one mystery had been solved. It dawned on us why Hank didn't attend the funeral—he was too busy packing up our house. He must have had a crew with a truck ready to haul everything away the moment we went to the service that morning. He had sold everything.

In some ways, we felt relieved not to be under his thumb. But didn't he have some obligation to us? What were we supposed to do now? We had no adults, no money, and no furniture, except for the Formica-top kitchen table—with no chairs. Someone decided to check the phone mounted on the kitchen wall. It worked. At least that was something. While the Hopes were too old to handle all of us, Kim said, "Is Aunt Penny someone who can help us?"

Mike took the lead. He placed the call, explained our situation, nodded a few times, and finally said, "That's okay, Aunt Penny, we understand, we'll figure something out...." My stomach started to sink. More bad news. Mike slowly returned the phone to its cradle. "Aunt Penny's husband, Bill, is dying of stomach cancer," he said. "She'd love to help, but under the circumstances it's not a good idea." He leaned against the doorjamb, head tilted back.

*Now what?*

I looked over at Mike. Something was eating at him. With a sigh, he said, "Look, guys, I hate to break this to you, especially with all that's going on. But I head back to Vietnam tomorrow. My furlough is only through midnight tonight. I've got to be back at the base this evening." Mike was assigned to the USS *Kansas City*, a giant ship assigned to refuel and rearm the battle groups. I had once visited, and now wished it would take me away too.

I sank to the floor. Who would take care of us, of me?

Mike started stuffing his things into his duffel bag. I knew he wasn't abandoning us. What choice did he have? Duty called. Still, the thought that he'd soon be leaving seemed to press the air out of my lungs. I pulled off my clip-on tie, tossed it on my pile of clothes, and headed for the door. I needed to get away from the chaos, if only for a minute.

Honestly, everyone was too busy trying to figure out what we were going to do to notice I was about to go outside. I didn't want anyone to show concern. I wandered off on my own most of the time anyway to ride my bike or play with friends. Nothing unusual about that. As I headed out the door, I heard Dave announce to the group, "Hey, I know a family that might take us in, at least for a while." He started to place the call as I closed the door behind me.

## A WALK TO REMEMBER

To say that I had been unprepared for the events of that day would be a gross understatement. It's as if the instant I got up that morning, I'd been swept away by a whirlwind of chaos. Seeing my dead mother's body. Watching my siblings cry. Standing by the grave. The parade of well-wishers. All of the talk about heaven. Seeing the stairs in the sky. Coming home to an empty house. Discovering that Hank had sold everything—and left us with nothing. Mike preparing to leave. Getting the news that Aunt Penny's husband was dying. How was I to make sense of it all?

Standing under the darkening sky, I hit rock bottom. I couldn't handle another thing. I was officially an orphan without a place to live or food to eat. And yet, at my absolute lowest, I remembered the flowers. What were they called?

Chrysanthemums.

I had completely forgotten about the chrysanthemums. The thought of them gave me a much-needed spark of hope. After all, Mom had asked me to plant them. It was our project, something just the two of us shared. I never told anyone about them, partly because it was personal and partly because I never gave them a second thought. But did they grow?

I had to find out.

I ran around the house to the flowerbed where, a few weeks before, I had so carefully planted them. As I approached, I didn't see anything at first. It was dark. For a second I wondered if I had the right spot. Getting down on one knee for a closer look, I was shocked that they were actually growing. I'd never planted anything in my life, and here they were; the first tiny sprouts pushing their way through the ground. While only an inch or two high, they were as wonderful to me as if they had been in full bloom. I kept thinking, *It worked. I must have planted them right!*

What a great confidence builder.

That's when a new idea struck me. When Mom had asked me to plant the flowers, she wasn't thinking of herself. They weren't for her enjoyment. She did it for my benefit. She must have known they'd become a living metaphor about life and new beginnings. It was almost as if she were saying, "Jimmy, I'm counting on you to carry on after I'm gone. Spring will come. The skies will brighten. You'll be just fine."

Whether or not that was what she had in mind, that's the impression the flowers had on me. On some deeper level, I also had a distinct spiritual impression that God was at work too. That even though Mom was gone, God was going to take care of me.

Resting on both knees, not caring that my corduroy pants were getting dirty, I tucked a few handfuls of earth around each of the plants. As I worked, I had a one-way chat with my mom. In my own childish way, I wanted to thank her for the flowers, for asking me to plant them, and for being such a great mom.

As I stood to leave, I debated digging up the flowers and taking them with us, but I didn't want them to die. I decided leaving them behind made more sense. I dusted my hands together, brushed the dirt from between my fingers, and headed for the door.

Rounding the corner of the house, I could see Dave, ear pressed against the phone, pacing the floor through the kitchen window. For the first time all day, I sensed that one way or the other, something would work out. We were due for a break. I walked in the door as Dave got off the phone all excited. He'd found us a place to stay. We were going to move in with the Reil family.

Life was about to get really weird.

6

# No Place Like Home

There's an old saying: *Home is where the heart is.* As sentimental catchphrases go, there's definitely a Norman Rockwell ring to it. I'd say it falls into the category of those timeless expressions best embroidered on a quilt draped over the back of a well-worn leather armchair next to a roaring fireplace.

*Home is where the heart is.*

Sure sounds nice, inviting, even cozy. I don't know who first penned the line. Maybe a writer for *The Saturday Evening Post*, or perhaps someone at Hallmark. But what if your heart has been drawn, quartered, and bruised beyond recognition? Where's home then? Our hearts were first broken when Dad and Mom separated. They were further splintered when Mom remarried, and finally shattered when she died. And even after all of that, Hank sold all of our possessions and left us penniless orphans.

*Home is where the heart is.*

On the night of Mom's funeral, home became anywhere we could find a place to lay our heads. Although Dave's phone call had yielded a place for us to stay, his friends lived more than a hundred miles east of Los Angeles. Dave decided that was too far to travel at such a late hour. Frankly, I was relieved. I wanted to hold on to what was left of my world as long as possible.

After Mike left for his ship, Dave, Dee Dee, Kim, and I made the best of our circumstances and settled in for the night. We huddled together on the carpeted floor in the living room. We had no pillows or blankets to pull over us, but at least we were together in our home. If I tried hard enough, I felt certain I could still smell Mom's perfume lingering in the hall.

I'm pretty sure Norman Rockwell would have never painted us sprawled out on the floor in the vacant room, with nothing but clothes in rumpled piles, doubling as cushions and blankets. Why capture the dark shadows of a nightmare when the world is filled with warmer, happier hues?

Besides, practically speaking, who wants to live like that? I didn't. Like Dorothy in *The Wizard of Oz*, I wanted to click my heels together three times and be instantly transported to the home I longed for … a place where laughter and good times were shared … where Mom and Dad teased each other with the snap of a kitchen towel after dinner … a place we once called home.

While the prospect of living with a family I didn't know wasn't my first choice, I took comfort in the fact that at least my siblings and I hadn't been split up like baggage at the airport, separated and sent to different final destinations. Unbelievably, that was a solution proposed by Hank a few days after Mom had died. In some of the most colorful tones I'd ever heard, Dave made it clear such a breakup would *never* happen.

With all of the talk about going to live with Dave's friends, the Reils, I couldn't help but wonder why we didn't go and live with Dad. Sure, he had problems, but maybe he had changed. He was still *my* dad, and I liked that option much better than stepping into the unknown. Of course, we hadn't seen him in years and had no idea where he was living, so that option wasn't really on the table.

Lying on the floor, eyelids at half-mast, my gaze was drawn to Mom's bedroom door. Part of me wanted to believe she'd walk out at any moment and call my name—that everything would be okay. What was she doing now that, according to Grandpa Hope, she was in heaven? Did people sleep in heaven? Could she see me missing her? Did she know how much I wanted to talk with her like before, to hear her voice again? Thankfully, Mr. Sandman rescued me from dwelling on what I no longer had.

## FORK IN THE ROAD

California's Interstate 10, locally known as the San Bernardino Freeway, is a twelve-lane, east/west concrete artery connecting Arizona to the Pacific Ocean. With Dave behind the wheel, Dee Dee riding shotgun, and Kim and I in the back, we drove eastward for what seemed like an eternity. Everything I had known—our house, my school, my friends, and Dad—was now a hundred miles away. Each passing mile separated me from the world I once knew and loved.

*Would I ever get to go back? Would I ever see my dad again?*

*Was that even possible?*

With my head against the window, I watched the trees and scrub brush whiz by in a blur of sameness. The rhythmic hum of tires over pavement put me in a trancelike state. I listened to the scratchy sounds emanating from the AM car radio: The Beatles wanted to hold someone's hand, the Monkees were believers, and Carol King was feeling the earth move under her feet—whatever that meant.

## Finding Home

Although sad to leave everything behind, I nevertheless felt safe and secure because my brother and sisters were with me. Even though Mom was gone and Mike was somewhere on the Pacific Ocean, I believed I could go anywhere and face anything as long as the rest of us stuck together. What's more, I was happy that Mike had promised to visit us one day when back at port. Maybe this change wouldn't be so difficult after all; at least that's what I told myself.

Every now and then I'd lean forward and rest my chin on the seat back for a better view. I was fascinated by the sporadic ping of bugs against glass, the windshield serving as their final resting place. I thought about how Mom would have joked, "Those bugs should have known better than to play tag with the windshield!"

With temperatures in the mideighties and without the luxury of air-conditioning in that car, we had to roll down the windows. I could feel the freeway bake with enough radiant energy to fry chicken, and maybe my face while it was at it. The sweltering air seemed reluctant to touch down where earth met sky, producing a hazy diffusion in the distance.

As if answering the unasked question endlessly circling my mind, Dave announced, "We're almost there." I fell back against my seat and resumed my watch for Route 62, also known as Twentynine Palms Highway. Although Dave was fully capable of the task, he had asked me to keep an eye out for our exit, probably to give me something to do. A sign announcing the city of Palm Springs came into view. Our exit was twelve miles away.

At the mention of Palm Springs, my sisters were quick to point out a laundry list of the famous celebrities who had a second home there … Clark Gable, Cary Grant, Steve McQueen, Donna Reed, Bob Hope, Liberace, and Frank Sinatra. They were names I didn't recognize, but the fact that they had a *second* home while we were homeless must have meant they were doing okay.

When someone mentioned that Elvis and Lucille Ball had houses there too, I understood we were talking about *really* famous people. People on TV. People like Larry from the Three Stooges. I'd later learn that Al Capone once used Suite 14 at the Two Bunch Palms resort to evade the police and rival thugs.

We passed the playground of the rich and famous and continued east toward Morongo Valley, a dry, dusty, barren stretch of land on the western edge of the Mojave Desert. Unlike Palm Springs, which had made the cover of *LIFE* magazine, Morongo Valley didn't have a shot at making the national news. After all, no movie stars lived there, at least none that Dee Dee and Kim knew about. In fact, with a population of less than 1,800, almost *nobody* lived there.

At least there was a family kind enough to take us in.

Dave exited onto Route 62 and followed the two-lane road north along the foothills of Mount San Gorgonio, a majestic 10,834-foot mass, the tallest mountain in Southern California. Living in the Long Beach basin, I'd forgotten how enormous it was. I craned my neck for a better view.

According to Dave, the rugged rock formations leading to the peak were the stomping grounds of bighorn sheep. I had hoped to catch a glimpse of those creatures, but the road parted company with the mountain and veered toward the high desert. The occasional patches of greenery on the foothills traded places with sagebrush, desert flora, and cacti that dotted the scorched earth.

Making a right turn onto T-Circle Drive, Dave gave us the skinny on the Reil family. They were, after all, our new house parents and we should know something about them. Vernon and Betty—Mr. and Mrs. Reil to us—were originally from Iowa and knew a thing or two about farming. They had four boys: David, nineteen; Paul, eighteen; Gary, fifteen; and Marky, age eight. Perhaps living with them might not be so bad.

Dave explained that Mr. Reil used to work as a butcher at the Hormel Foods Corporation meatpacker plant in Osceola, Iowa. He and the other meat cutters would butcher a hog, and then place various cuts of pork onto iron gaffing hooks. Like a mini-monorail, the hooks hauled the meat overhead on a track system to the next station to turn it into Spam, Black Label Ham, or one of their other signature products. Evidently, one of the hooks broke, dropping a hefty side of pork on Mr. Reil, and three discs in his neck were ruptured.

With Mr. Reil disabled and unable to continue working at the meat plant, the Reils moved west and somehow stumbled onto a five-acre lot at the end of T-Circle Drive. There, Mr. Reil and his boys built chicken coops, rabbit cages, and goat pens. The Reils raised their own fruits and vegetables and lived off the land. That sounded pretty neat. I pictured their family as modern-day pioneers; Mr. Reil probably had a lot in common with Davy Crockett or maybe Paul Bunyan. You know, a burly, salt-of-the-earth, lumberjack type.

Almost on cue, Dave shattered my impression when he added that Mr. Reil had had three heart attacks, was a chain-smoker, and took nitroglycerine. I wasn't sure how much I was supposed to read between the lines. Did that mean Mr. Reil might die any day? What if he had a stroke while we were there? I was quick to push the questions out of my mind, having dealt with enough thoughts about death to last a lifetime.

Dave slowed the car and his narration as the pavement abruptly yielded to a bumpy dirt road. A row of rusted mailboxes perched on crooked wooden posts marked the transition from civilization to the wild frontier. After navigating several miles of car-eating craters, we reached a deep, wide channel cut into the earth—what country folk call a "wash" since your car or truck or whatever would sometimes have to wade through water to reach the bank of the other side.

We drove down into the wash, which happened to be dry, and, maybe thirty yards later, ascended the dirt road on the other side. I inched forward in my seat as we crested the incline. My heart hammered away as the Reils' private plateau came into view. Nothing Dave might have said could have prepared me for the scene unfolding before us. This wasn't Palm Springs. Not even close. By all appearances, we had entered a dimension closer to the *Twilight Zone*.

## ALL IN THE FAMILY

Dave leaned on the accelerator as we ascended the embankment from the wash. Free-range chickens squawked and leaped, startled by our sudden appearance. Feathers flapping, they made a mad dash for the safety of the henhouse on our left. Brownish-gray planks of wood, bleached by the unmerciful sun, appeared to have been haphazardly tacked together to construct the enclosure.

Adjacent to the chicken coop, a large wood stump with an ax stuck in the flat top caught my attention. Red-brown streaks stained the top and sides of the stump clearly suggesting blood. What else could it be? In true city-slicker fashion, I thought: *Do they really chop off chicken heads? I could never do that.*

The pea-gravel crunching beneath our tires announced our approach. Dave followed the circular driveway toward the house on the opposite end. A vegetable garden sprouted in the center of the private turnaround drive. Hunched over, Mr. Reil was fussing at the ground with a hoe. Slim as a scarecrow, he was no more than 5'6" and maybe 145 pounds. With a turn, he straightened up and offered a smile and a wave. With no visible teeth, his lips seemed to pucker inward as if curling over his gums. I'd later learn he did own, but rarely wore, his dentures.

Scanning the yard beyond him, I saw the skeletons of several vehicles in various stages of disrepair, hoods raised, resting either on cinder blocks, or crouched on the ground with a platoon of weeds holding the tires captive. I would soon learn that the picked-over carcasses of the cars, trucks, or tractors deemed unsalvageable ended up in the ravine where the Reils dumped their trash.

The ravine was no more than fifteen feet from the back of the house and just beyond the clothesline. Running north to south, the gorge, while not particularly deep, had to be the width of two football fields. Without trash service, the Reils apparently decided to conduct their own landfill operation by tossing in their daily garbage, as well as busted chairs, auto parts, paint cans, animal carcasses, and whatnot. I'm fairly sure they didn't have government approval for that.

On the far end of the circular drive, Dave rolled to a stop in front of the one-story house, a square, cinder-block structure with a flat roof. Their home wasn't what I had pictured at all. The house had been painted pink, the color of Pepto-Bismol, or perhaps a little more like Barbie Doll pink. Given the choice of house color, I wouldn't have been surprised to see a clutch of plastic flamingos staked in the flowerbeds.

An enclosed patio jutted off the rear of the house, which, I'd soon learn, was where six of us—the four Reil brothers and Dave and I—would sleep on beds lined up in a row like an army barrack. Did I mention that the cramped, makeshift room was well within sniffing distance of the decomposing trash in the ravine?

Their house was a patchwork of poorly constructed additions as Mr. Reil annexed the outdoors to make more living space. Let me just say he appeared long on ideas but short on talent when it came to being a carpenter. I doubt a building inspector ever set foot in the house, because there's no way the ragtag workmanship would have been approved.

A short, stocky woman appeared by the screen door. She wore a loose-fitting muumuu dress and unlaced sneakers. Her hair was pulled back into a matted ponytail. "That's Mrs. Reil," Dave said, turning off the car and stepping out. I followed, though somewhat reluctantly. Like a master of ceremonies, Dave launched into a series of introductions. When my turn came, I shook Mrs. Reil's hand, which felt weathered like leather.

At least she didn't pinch my cheek.

A stale, ripe smell emanated from within the house, like a locker room overdue for a good hosing down. And, as I'd come to find out, with just one bathroom, no bathtub, one shower, one sink, and a toilet to serve twelve people, personal hygiene became a contest of wills.

Was staying with my dad really out of the question?

Carrying armloads of clothes from the car, we started to settle in our new shared home. We brought no possessions with us because Hank had sold everything—including my blue Stingray bike. In some respects, the fact that we had no furniture was probably a good thing considering how tiny the house was. The Reils had been crowded with six people; with us, that number swelled to ten.

To say that our time living with the Reil family was "strange" would be kind. More accurately, if *Ripley's Believe It or Not!* were to list the most bizarre places to live, the Reil home would probably be close to the top. While thankful for a roof over my head, it didn't take me long to wonder: *So ... where did Dave meet these people?*

Don't get me wrong. The first couple of weeks were relatively "normal" as we adapted to each other, to our new surroundings, and to my new school. I was sent to the only school in Morongo Valley, Morongo Valley Elementary School. Since it was March and the school year was well on its way, I entered the fourth-grade class and did what I could to fit into the existing cliques.

On the homefront, learning the Reils' daily routine was actually rather simple since it rarely changed. Every morning was like a scene from Bill Murray's *Groundhog Day*. While we kids jockeyed for a few precious minutes of privacy in the bathroom, Mrs. Reil made breakfast. She would toast up a loaf of bread and mix a vat of instant hot chocolate, occasionally adding a hint of goats milk. She'd sprinkle cinnamon and sugar on the toast, and stack the slices on a plate. Everyone dipped the toast into his or her hot chocolate.

The breakfast menu never changed.

We always had cinnamon toast and hot chocolate.

For variety, some days we had hot chocolate … and cinnamon toast. With all of the chickens running around, I wondered why we didn't have eggs at least once in a while. I can't recall ever drinking a glass of milk. No wonder I broke so many bones when I reached high school. We also never prayed before eating. Hank the Tank would have been miffed. I had grown accustomed to giving thanks for our food and missed that practice.

After dinner came a ritual that I observed, but never participated in. Their idea of a good time was to gather around the kitchen table to talk and smoke, smoke and talk, night after night, all the while rolling endless batches of cigarettes. Even Gary and Paul smoked and rolled cigarettes with their parents. While Marky didn't smoke, he helped with the manufacturing process. The table, with a Formica top and tubular metal legs, became their workbench.

With a "thunk," Mrs. Reil would place a large tin of tobacco on the table, fetch a cache of rolling papers and filters, and then pull up a chair. Using a cigarette roller machine they all took turns loading the paper, the filter, and then the tobacco. For its part, the machine whirled with a "chi chi" sound and, moments later, spat out a perfectly rolled cigarette. I was never tempted to try one of those things … it just seemed not too smart to smoke it.

While they worked, the AM radio blared away in the corner. Either they couldn't afford a television, or didn't have reception out in the boondocks, because the radio provided our only entertainment. After dark, the stations in the area signed off until sunup, and when the signal faded, we called it a night. After all, it was pitch black outside with no streetlights and no neighbors for at least a mile.

I think we might have been able to handle living with the Reils if hot chocolate and toast for breakfast, and rolling cigarettes listening to AM radio at night, had been the extent of their weirdness. Far from it. During the course of the one year we were in their foster care, for example, David Reil, who was nineteen, decided to marry his forty-two-year-old cousin. Even at ten years of age, I knew that was kind of strange.

And that wasn't the half of it. For the Reils, life was a never-ending, convoluted sitcom.

## RUN, CHICKEN, RUN

Every culture on earth has a rite of passage. In various African tribes, when a boy turns thirteen, the men assemble and hand him his first hunting spear. In Jewish tradition, a thirteen-year-old boy is given a bar mitzvah, a ceremony recognizing him as an adult member of the community. Catholics experience this rite of passage through the process of confirmation.

Some see significant events in life as a rite of passage: a toddler's first haircut, a young woman who starts wearing makeup, or a young man who has his first shave. A first girlfriend or boyfriend, a first cigarette, or enduring college hazing are milestones signifying a transition in life. I discovered the Reil family's version of a rite of passage one Saturday morning several weeks into our stay.

After a hearty breakfast of hot chocolate and cinnamon toast, Mr. Reil rounded up Marky, Gary, and me, and we headed for the chicken coop. I figured we were just going to collect some more of the eggs that we never ate at breakfast. Reaching the henhouse, Mr. Reil lit up a cigarette and surveyed the coop with a practiced eye. He took a long, unhurried drag, pointed to a plump bird, exhaled a cloud of smoke, and told Gary to bring the unfortunate specimen to the wood stump.

I knew full well that the meat we ate came from the chickens, rabbits, and goats raised by the Reils. I just wasn't around for the killing, which was fine by me. With the exception of swatting flies or stomping spiders, I'd never killed anything in my life.

Before I knew what was happening, Mr. Reil, in full butcher mode, had a chicken pinned down on the chopping block, neck exposed. In one smooth, effortless swing, he knocked its head off. The headless chicken flopped to the ground and took off running. Watching it flail about was as unnerving as anything you might read in a sci-fi novel. For a good five minutes, the chicken staggered around and bumped into things, blood squirting out of its artery like a fountain. I backed away as it did a few headless flips. That was a new experience for me.

About the time the bird ran out of nervous energy, I heard Mr. Reil call my name. Marky, with a smirk I'll not forget, readily produced another chicken. Like he was initiating some sort of rite of passage, Mr. Reil held out the handle of the ax for me to take. Speaking through puckered gums, he said, "Jimmy, it's your turn to cut off the head." The look in his eye implied this was a command not a suggestion.

Right. As if I wanted to do that.

I hesitated.

Mr. Reil puffed away with his left hand while extending the ax to me in his right. Everything about his stance seemed to say, "Son, I have all the time in the world. You can either take this ax and get 'er done, or fret for a few hours. But we'll not leave this place until you take the head off of that bird. Suit yourself."

I stole a look at Gary and Marky who were having a total kick over my anxiety. They knew that their dad was the law in these parts. This was his land. His house. Mr. Reil was both the judge and the supreme court of the valley. I didn't have any option but to comply. There wasn't a higher authority to appeal to, and not wanting to end up like the headless hen, I stepped forward and took the ax.

I raised the blade and held my breath. It was one thing to eat chicken and quite another to do the deed. Time seemed to move in slow motion. While I felt sorry for the hen, I didn't want to miss and embarrass myself in front of them. I winced and let the ax fall. With my eyes partially closed, I felt the ax connect with a "Whomp!"

I'm not sure how I managed to hit the neck. But I did. With its head successfully lopped off, the chicken took off running, leaving a trail of blood everywhere—on the stump, the ax ... even on my pant leg. I didn't spend a lot of time going back to the chicken coop after I cut that chicken's head off. I'm sure the Reils had a good laugh at my discomfort during supper. My only defense was to tune them out and withdraw into the safety of my own little world. I picked at my plate and went to bed hungry.

The mood between our families began to change not long after that incident. A clear line in the sand was being drawn, with their kids on one side, and us on the other. Things got so strained that Kim ran off not long afterward and married a guy, probably to put some distance between herself and the Reils' wild and wacky world.

That left Dave, Dee Dee, and me to take the brunt of the antics of this household. Well, mostly Dee Dee and me since Dave was gone most of the time at work.

Two brief examples come to mind. Marky, whom I originally had hopes of befriending, turned out to be a closet kleptomaniac. He liked stealing my stuff, what little I had to my name. He'd take things from the bundle that I kept under my cot and then stash the items in his dresser drawer. When confronted, Marky would deny it.

When I'd go to Mrs. Reil to explain what was going on, Marky would say, "I didn't steal from him—he's a lying pig." She just shook her head and took his side. Mrs. Reil would say, "Not *our* Marky. You must be wrong, Jimmy. Your problem is that you lose things and want to blame someone for it. No, it's not Marky." Years later, long after we were gone and Marky had turned eighteen, I heard that he was sent to the state penitentiary for fraud and forgery. I wonder how his life might have turned out differently had he been taught to own his "stuff," like my mom taught me.

I could deal with Marky pilfering my stuff and lying to my face to cover his tracks. What was a bit more difficult was discovering that Gary was a homosexual who looked at me in ways I didn't understand at the time. Keep in mind I had just turned ten—a birthday the Reils didn't even celebrate. I never had "The Talk" about sex with either of my parents. To me, girls still had cooties.

Imagine my surprise when Gary, who was five years older than me, started to take an interest in me. I'd come in from playing in the canyon looking for lizards and such, eat dinner, and then hear Gary say, "Hey, you're kinda cute." He approached me about his desires, but nothing happened. Frankly, it struck me as odd. Apparently, a little resistance was enough to keep him at bay.

I was in a no-win situation. After the way the Reils turned a deaf ear to my concerns about Marky's stealing, I knew they'd brush me off if I told them about Gary. I could hear Mrs. Reil say, "Not *our* Gary. This must be your problem. Maybe *you're* the one who is attracted to men, Jimmy."

I'd pull the covers tight and hope my brother Dave would hurry home from work. Dave had been working two jobs at the time just to give us a little spending money. Thoughts of finding and moving in with my dad resurfaced. Anything had to be better than unwanted sexual advances. No kid should have to face that.

Thankfully, God heard the cry of my heart, and nothing physical ever happened between us. When it was clear that I had no intention of becoming Gary's special friend, he didn't hassle me as often. Nevertheless, the tensions between the Reil family and us continued to increase. It was a matter of time before something bad was bound to happen.

## YOU'RE KILLING ME

Although the entire Reil family was melodramatic, no one could top Gary. He bled drama. If Gary stubbed his toe, the whole family would panic and say, "We've got to rush Gary to the hospital—they may have to amputate his leg." Gary would lock himself in the bathroom and threaten to kill himself with a bottle of aspirin over the slightest infraction.

Such vaudeville theatrics seemed more pronounced and more frequent as summer ended and the fall rolled around. The crowded conditions of the house, the fights over who got to use the one bathroom, the body odor and stale smell of smoke hanging in the air—no wonder everyone was nuts.

By then, Mr. Reil joined the act with his own histrionics. Somehow he got the idea in his head that someone was trying to kill him. I learned about his paranoia during a meeting with the social worker assigned to supervise our case.

We'd been at the Reils' for six months when she dropped by for the first visit and professional evaluation. While I don't remember her name, I do recall she was about thirty years old and had a winsome smile. Dave and I sat across from her at the kitchen table. Apparently, she'd already met with the Reils and now it was our turn. Hooking her hair behind her left ear, she smiled again, and said, "Look, I think we have a problem."

I'm thinking, *Yeah, tell me about it.... This place is crazy.*

She lowered her voice a notch and added, "Mr. Reil said that you tried to kill him."

I shot my brother a look. "Dave?!"

Before Dave could respond, she said, "No, Jimmy, Mr. Reil claims *you* tried to kill him."

"Me?"

She nodded, slowly.

It was Dave's turn to be surprised. "Jimmy?!"

"But ... I'm ten years old!"

Was everybody losing their mind? I was sure Dave knew that I wasn't capable of killing anything—except for flies, spiders, and now chickens. I was a harmless wallflower. Would this lady believe me? Or, would she take sides with the Reils and just send me off to jail? I wasn't even sure whether social workers could send people to jail. About all I could say in my defense was ... "How?"

She leaned forward, raised an eyebrow, and said, "Mr. Reil claims you tried to push him off of a cliff."

"You're serious?" I mean, this was one of those ten-year-old observations: *We were living in the desert.* There were no cliffs for miles. Sure, there was the ravine out back, but that was more of a gentle slope. At best I might have been able to roll Mr. Reil down there to join all of the stuff they'd been dumping for years. But it was definitely not a cliff. I just wasn't sure if my view would hold up in court.

The lady cleared her throat. "Yes, that's what he said. Which is also why Mr. Reil has been sleeping in the rabbit hutch for several days."

*So that's what he's been doing out there,* I thought. My heart started bumping around in my chest like, well, like a chicken with its head missing. She must have perceived my growing panic. With a smile, she winked. In the following minutes, she explained that she thought Mr. Reil was going senile.

She said, "There really are just two options. First, we can keep you guys together and you can hunker down here until we find another solution. If so, I'll do what I can to make sure Mr. Reil understands you don't mean him any harm. Or, we can separate you and place you into the appropriate foster-care homes for your respective ages."

I didn't like the sound of either of those options. In my view, there was a third idea: find Dad and live with him. Hands down, that was my first choice. But we still didn't know where to find Dad, and Dave and Dee Dee were unconvinced that move was wise. Not wanting to break up the family, we agreed to stay for another six months. While that decision made the most sense at the time, a fresh round of trouble was just around the corner.

The Reils invited another family to move in.

# 7

# The Prowlers

Being falsely accused of attempted murder at age ten is not the kind of thing a boy easily shakes off. The memory of sitting with the social worker as she broke the news that Mr. Reil thought I was trying to kill him had a significant impact on me. Her visit lingered in my mind long after she snapped her thin, padded briefcase and drove off to the next foster-care case.

She was nice enough to believe me, which I was thankful for. Still, the encounter felt as if I had received a summons to report to the principal's office for some wrongdoing that I had no part in, like spraying graffiti on the bathroom wall. My guilt or innocence wasn't the issue. The fact that I was *accused* marked me as someone to watch.

Where there's smoke there's fire, right?

Try though I did, I couldn't fathom what fiendish act I could have committed that would have given Mr. Reil a reason to think I wanted to kill him. I didn't harass him. I didn't joke about tearing him apart, limb from limb. I didn't even have those feelings so it wasn't as if he could read something between the lines. I was about as threatening as a houseplant. The social worker apparently said something to Mr.

Reil before she left that calmed him. He stopped sleeping in the rabbit hutch, but still, I felt watched, as if on probation.

From that day forward, my best defense was to stay far away from the Reils whenever possible—no small task given how cramped the house was. Like sardines, we marinated in each other's space. After school, I kept out of sight by playing in the ravine. However, once the sun went down, my options were limited. I found the best idea was to retreat to my bed before the others called it a night. That worked for a while—at least until the prowlers showed up.

One evening, long after the sun had called it quits for the day, I was lying on my cot out on the enclosed patio staring at a network of cobwebs where the ceiling met the house. Although Mrs. Reil was constantly doing laundry, she rarely attended to things like the spider webs overhead or the dust bunnies on the concrete floor. I'm not faulting her; she simply didn't have time to be Suzie Housekeeper.

That's understandable considering how much effort went into washing clothes for ten people, especially with one of those prehistoric washing machines. Mrs. Reil had the kind of antiquated device that sported two top-mounted, hand-cranked rollers that, when turned, squeezed the excess water out. Sort of a manual spin cycle. Then, she'd hang the clothes out to line-dry. The process took forever.

That night, the cobwebs failed to provide enough action to hold my attention. I couldn't find a moth or unlucky fly struggling to break free before a spider came for his dinner. Bored, I decided to go to sleep. I wanted to read a comic book, but I didn't have one. We were never given any spending money, and even if I had a dime, there were no stores within walking distance.

I rolled off the cot, careful not to bang my knees on the adjacent bed less than a foot away. I crossed the room and turned off the lamp. Slipping back under the covers, I looked out the window. It didn't take long for my eyes to adjust to the darkness and for the stars to come into view. That was one of the great things about living in the desert—the sky is so clear. The stars seem to gleam like a freshly washed chrome bumper in the sun.

Against the backdrop of the night sky, the Big Dipper and its galactic companions generated enough light to cast a soft bluish glow against the windowpane. September had brought with it slightly cooler evening temperatures; the clean, cool air carried with it the scent of desert flora that drifted through my partially opened window.

I could hear the Reils swapping stories in the adjacent room, but tuned them out in favor of my own thoughts. School was back in session. While the kids in my fifth-grade class were nice enough, I didn't feel particularly connected to them. I was still very much the new kid in town without a shared history. I missed my friends back in Long Beach.

Lost in my reflection about what the new school year might hold, I heard, or thought I heard, approaching footsteps. The enclosed patio walls were thin and, most likely, not insulated—something similar to plywood, painted pale green on the inside, tacked to two-by-four wooden posts. Sound traveled easily through the flimsy exterior surface. The barking of a dog or the closing of a car door a mile away sounded as if it were nearby.

The fact that someone might be walking out there in the dark was unusual. The Reils rarely had visitors, and never at this hour. I listened more carefully. Nothing. Maybe I had been mistaken. Or, maybe it hadn't been human footsteps. Perhaps a goat had weaseled out of its pen and was heading to the garbage dump for a late-night snack. No. There it was again, the distinct sound of soles against gravel, moving toward the house.

I sat upright, but didn't approach the window. My pulse quickened, more out of curiosity than fear. That is, until I perceived another set of footsteps. Two visitors? Or, were there three?

Definitely more than one. The number was hard to distinguish over the accelerated thumping in my chest. Were they friendly visitors? Guests? The Reils hadn't mentioned they were expecting company. I'm pretty sure they would have said something.

How would anybody find this place? The house wasn't visible from the main dirt access road until you drove down through the wash and up the other side. That was odd. I didn't hear a car pull up. I ruled out the possibility that it might be one or more of the Reils in the yard. When I had left the kitchen, everyone was accounted for. They'd taken up their usual seats around the table and were busy rolling cigarettes. If someone had stepped out, I would have heard the screen door smack the doorjamb.

These footsteps were slow and tentative. They were not the bold, confident steps of someone who lived there and knew the place like the back of their hand. Whoever they were, and whatever their business, I decided they had no good reason to be out there.

When the face appeared in the window, I stopped breathing.

## WATCH AND PREY

The trespasser wore a black ski mask pulled taut across his face—the kind used by bank robbers. Only this wasn't a bank, and we had no money. With the exception of two slits for the eyes, and one for the mouth, his features were concealed. I quickly ruled out the idea that this was a surprise visit from an old friend. I was equally sure he wasn't a representative from the Morongo Valley Welcome Wagon finally coming around to greet us kids.

The spike pinning my heart against my rib cage assured me this wasn't a dream. I was very much awake wishing it *were* a nightmare. That's the thing about bad dreams. In even the most terrible nightmares, you always survived. In real life, the outcome was always up for grabs.

A large masked face blocked the spot in the window where I had been watching the Big Dipper. With less than five feet between us, I dared not move. Could he see me? My room was dark and the blanket covered my legs, but I was sitting upright on the bed. Maybe he was allowing his eyes to adjust to the interior darkness, or perhaps my face had been briefly illuminated by the moon's glow and he was deciding what to do next.

But he just waited. And stared.

I fully expected him to slip a gloved hand through the gap at the bottom of the window and nudge it open farther. If so, then what? For a second, I debated reaching forward to slam the window shut. However, if he *didn't* know I was there, such brashness would be a dead giveaway that the room was occupied. And, come to think of it, I wasn't even sure that the window lock worked.

Afraid that any sound might betray my position, I remained as mute as a stone sculpture. Even the slightest movement on the bed would provoke the rickety, steel-spring mesh beneath the mattress to squeak. I felt as if I were sitting on live dynamite. Although frozen in place, my mind sped through the options. Should I scream? Run for help? Stand my ground?

More footsteps approached. The intruder turned his head in the direction of his partner. I used the momentary distraction to breathe. His head rotated back and then he looked at me. I was convinced he *knew* I was there. Alone. I didn't know whether or not he was armed and dangerous, or just intent on terrorizing us for fun. I didn't care to find out. An exchange of muffled voices broke his stare and, seconds later, drew him from his post by my window.

But for how long?

My stunned silence gave way to a gasp. There was no time to waste. With a sharp tug, I ripped the blanket off of my legs, popped up from the bed like a jack-in-the-box, and cracked my right knee against the metal frame of Dave's cot. I winced, but managed to stay standing, then backed away from the window where the black figure once stood. Stubbing my toe on some unseen object left on the floor by the baseboard, I found the doorknob and, with a yank, pulled the door open.

I burst into the kitchen, yelling, "They're out there! They're out there! Two or three men!" The conversation stopped as everyone looked up at the crazy kid in the doorway. For a moment, nobody spoke. Mr. Reil blew a steady stream of smoke through his nose. His eyebrows knotted into a brown wrinkle. With a squint, he looked at me as if I had grown two heads. Bewildered at what might have come over me, he said, "Slow down, sonny. What men?"

Didn't he hear what I just said? I pointed back toward the patio door. "Some guy … with a black mask … in my window … staring right at me!" Mr. Reil reached up with his left hand and stroked his chin. Head tilted to the side, he stared at me as if I were speaking Russian. When nobody moved to check out my story, I said, "There were more, too."

"More what?" Marky asked, toying with me. "More of your little dreams?"

I felt my face flush. I knew what he was doing. He was comparing this to the time when I had accused him of stealing my stuff. Siding with Marky, Mrs. Reil insisted I had imagined the whole thing. She didn't believe me then, why should she—or anyone—believe me now? My credibility was zero with this bunch.

"More bad guys. And I wasn't dreaming, Marky."

I stood there like Paul Revere sounding the alarm, while the sleepy townspeople paid no attention to the warning. What reason would I have to lie about something like this? On the off chance I was right, wouldn't it make sense to find out if, indeed, we were in some sort of imminent danger? How could they be so dismissive? I knew my brother Dave would have backed me up, but he was working third shift at the Circle K.

Gary who, at times, was a great conversationalist, was also the original Mr. Theatrics. Breaking the silence, Gary said, "Jimmy, are you sure you aren't hallucinating? Or maybe exaggerating just to get some attention?"

"You can see for yourself," I started to say, when Marky cut me off.

"Why don't you just go back to bed, Jimmy." Marky's contempt was as thick as the gray cloud of cigarette smoke hanging in the air. I can't say I ever met another eight-year-old with so much raw hostility. Reasoning with him was pointless. Invariably, he'd just call me a liar, or worse.

I wasn't sure if I was more hurt or angry that not one person believed me. I *knew* what I saw—the masked face was not my imagination. And, no, this wasn't some game to get noticed. I didn't want attention—certainly not from them. In fact, I was doing my best to avoid them. If they didn't care about the prowlers, fine.

As I turned to leave, my sister Dee Dee left the naysayers behind and followed me out of the kitchen. As we took a seat in another room, she slipped her arm around my shoulder. Pulling me close, she said, "It's okay, Jimmy. I believe you. If you want, you can sleep in my room tonight. Don't listen to them."

That was easier said than done. I could overhear Marky and Gary mimicking me in the other room, embellishing my words as if I were certifiably nuts.... *"They're out there! Run for your lives! Yeah, watch out for the men in masks. They've come to take us away!"*

Sitting with my sister helped insulate me from their ridicule. A variety of verbal jabs came to mind, but I didn't say a thing. My mother didn't raise me that way. She was fond of saying, "Treat others the way you want to be treated, Jimmy," and for that reason, I held my tongue.

To say that I withdrew into my own world after that experience wouldn't be accurate. To be withdrawn implies I wasn't connected to reality. I was connected. I just didn't like what I was connected to. Like Alice in Wonderland, I wanted to be free of that strange house, these strange people, and especially these strange happenings.

## SHOWDOWN AT SUNDOWN

The rest of the evening and throughout the next day, I was the resident joke. I was the crazy kid who had cried wolf … that is, until the howling started. The prowlers who supposedly didn't exist began circling the house once again, this time yelping like hungry coyotes. For a short moment, the Reils suspended their cigarette rolling and fell deathly silent. The noise in the yard couldn't be dismissed as my imagination run wild, and they knew it.

Not that anyone offered an apology.

When several masked faces darted past the kitchen window, it was Gary's and Marky's turn to become melodramatic. "What are we gonna do?" "We're all gonna die!" "Somebody call 911!" Mr. Reil pulled the curtain closed and told his sons to knock it off, adding, "I can't think above your racket, daggumit."

After much animated debate, they decided that they couldn't ignore the problem. Something had to be done. The Reils weren't about to be intimidated by these hoodlums. A show of force was necessary. This was their land, and they'd defend it like Davy Crockett's last stand at the Alamo. David Reil volunteered to play the part of Davy Crockett.

I wasn't so sure that was a good idea. I mean, what did he plan to do once he was outside? What if these guy were armed? We had no idea why they'd come, what they wanted, or how many bad guys were circling the house. What was David going to do against two, three, or more men?

Besides, I didn't think the Reils understood the severity of getting involved with thugs. I knew from my Compton days that sometimes these things ended up really bad—as in yellow chalk outlining the position of a dead body. Personally, I would have called and waited for the police—not that anybody was asking for my opinion.

By the sound of the screeching, the trespassers were in the backyard running in several directions. Flashlight in hand, David Reil, Righter of Wrongs, stepped out the door. Within two minutes, the whooping stopped. As far as we could tell, nobody had heard David shouting at the bad guys to get off of the property. There hadn't been the sounds of a struggle—you know, grunting, groaning, things smashing, and the like.

With a click, Mr. Reil snapped off the radio for a more careful listen. Aside from the barking of a dog, we heard nothing unusual. No footsteps. No movement outside. And no David. Just an uneasy stillness. Had David somehow scared them off just by his presence? Had he chased them to the edge of the property? If so, where was he? Why hadn't he returned? What was taking him so long?

The silence was deafening.

Several more tense minutes passed, and still no David. Not a peep from the prowlers, either. Agitated, Gary got up from the table and paced the floor. "We can't just sit here. What if David's dead? Huh? What if they kidnapped him—did you think of that? I just *knew* he shouldn't have gone after them."

Although not as dramatic, Mrs. Reil agreed. "Maybe you should do somethin', Vernon." She tucked a cigarette between her lips, struck a match, and lit up.

From left to right: Jim, DeeDee, Mike, Dave, and Kim in front of the Cosby house

Grandma and Grandpa Hope

My mom, Jan Daly

My siblings and I -
top: Kim; bottom from left to right: Mike, Jim, DeeDee, and Dave

May 2007 - left to right:
Jim, DeeDee, Mike, Kim,
and Dave

Mike in Navy

Jim Daly - 2nd grade

The meeting at the Reils
-from left to right:
Mike, Dad, Jim, DeeDee,
and Dave

Standing by the front door, Mr. Reil scratched the back of his head. "Like what?"

"Like … maybe go find David?" she said.

"Aw, he's a big boy, he's fine."

"He's a kid."

"He's nineteen, Betty," Mr. Reil said. "He can handle himself, otherwise he wouldn't be out there."

She tapped the end of her cigarette into the ashtray with a yellowed finger. "I'm just saying, he might need a hand, that's all."

"Yeah, Dad," Gary said, plopping back down in a chair. "Why don't you go get yourself killed too."

With a wave of her hand, dismissing his concern as overblown, Mrs. Reil said, "Gary, come on now … nobody's gonna get killed."

Gary rolled his eyes. "But, Mom, how do you know they're not escapees from death row or something, huh?"

Mr. Reil had had enough. Without a word, he reached for the front door and started to leave. Crossing the threshold and walking out a few yards, he stopped in his tracks.

"Whatcha see, Vernon?" Mrs. Reil said, leaning forward.

"I found David."

Gary and Marky jetted to the door before Mrs. Reil could free herself from her chair. Mr. Reil held up a hand, palm forward, like a policeman directing traffic, stopping them at the door. "Back inside, Marky. Gary, stand there and hold the door."

"Not fair," Marky said.

"Go! Now! Let Mom through."

I kept my distance. I couldn't really hear what was going on outside, between Marky's protests and Gary, as Gary held the screen door open with an arm, whining, "He's dead, right? I *knew* he was dead.... I told you, but you didn't listen to me!"

Mr. and Mrs. Reil struggled to support David's weight as they carried their son through the door; Mr. Reil's arms cradled his neck and back while Mrs. Reil lugged his limp legs. They laid him on the sofa in the living room. That's when I saw the side of David's head was covered in matted blood. Moving faster than I'd ever seen her move before, Mrs. Reil grabbed two washcloths, filled one with ice, and dipped the other in water. As she tended to the wound, Mr. Reil straightened and said, "He ain't dead, just unconscious."

"Not dead? He's not dead?" Gary gasped in relief.

"No. Just a nasty cut. Got walloped with a plank of wood, or maybe a pipe. Probably needs stitches," Mr. Reil said, taking a seat. Although he sounded surprisingly composed, I could tell by his knotted forehead that he was shaken up.

Lying prone on the couch, David groaned. Mrs. Reil held the ice, wrapped in the washcloth, to David's head. "Shh. Don't move. Just lay there, Son."

"So, why aren't we taking him to the hospital?" Marky asked.

Mr. Reil said, "No car."

"What! Where's the car?" Gary said, panicked. "He needs a doctor or he's gonna die."

"Betcha Bill's got it, right?" Marky said.

Mr. Reil nodded. About a week before the prowlers arrived, the Reils took in Bill Appletree, a full-blooded Native American Indian, along with his wife, their infant, and pint-size dog. The already crowded house, now with thirteen people, was an unbearably cramped circus. I never found out where Mr. Reil met Bill, or why he invited his family to stay with us.

Bill was on the heavy side. His shoulder-length black hair was as straight and as fine as silk. He wore a leather bandanna around his head and sported several turquoise-colored rings. His eyes were as intense as a storm and seemed to hide a dark secret. Privately, my brother Dave and I nicknamed him "Wild Bill."

Bill's wife was blonde, fair skinned, heavyset, and almost never spoke—at least not in front of us. Her time was consumed by doting on their infant. Almost from the minute they arrived, Bill spent virtually all of his time rebuilding the engine of his red Pontiac GTO. While he didn't give us a reason to be afraid of him, his friends spooked us—at least, we assumed they were his friends. Throughout the day, the biker-guys, as Dee Dee and I called them, would show up to talk to Wild Bill.

These were characters from the rough end of the spectrum. Festooned in chains and black leather jackets with skulls and cross-bones plastered on the back, they'd rumble into the yard as if they owned the place. One biker, with a bushy handlebar mustache, got his kicks hitting on my sister Dee Dee.

"Gee, that was dumb, Dad." Marky was speaking. "Why'd you give Bill *our* car?"

Mr. Reil sat hunched forward, resting his forearms on his legs. He appeared drained and in need of his heart pills. When he didn't imme-diately answer, Marky said, "Oh, wait … let me guess, he needed parts for his piece-o'-junk car. Is that it?"

"Leave him be, Marky," Mrs. Reil said.

"You know, none of this crazy stuff happened until Bill got here," Gary said, pointing toward Bill's bedroom. "I bet he ripped off one of those biker friends of his."

"They're Hells Angels," Marky replied.

"Hell's Bells, hippies on wheels, call 'em what you want." Gary started pacing again. "Nope. We never had prowlers until you took in those people."

"Hush your mouth, Gary," Mrs. Reil said.

"Well, it's true."

Mr. Reil lifted his head. "You heard her. Shut your trap."

The kitchen screen door opened and closed with a *thwack*. Wild Bill tossed the keys on the kitchen counter, plucked a cigarette from the stack on the table, and tucked it over his right ear. With wide strides, he paraded through the living room and headed straight for his sleeping wife and child in the back bedroom.

Marky blurted, "Hey, where've you been?"

"Out. What's it to you?" Wild Bill stopped long enough to answer, apparently unaware of David's condition.

"Only that David is dying." Gary pointed toward the couch.

"He's not dying," Mrs. Reil said. "But he needs a doctor. Vernon, give me a hand already."

Bill surveyed the situation and glided to David's side. "Here, let me." His thick arms lifted David from the couch effortlessly. Heading toward the kitchen, Bill said over his shoulder, "Who did this?"

Marky and Gary spoke almost in unison: "The prowlers." Over breakfast that morning, Bill had listened without speaking as the boys made a big joke about the masked man in my window. At the time, I couldn't tell whether Bill believed them or me. He just maintained a faraway look, as if deep in thought.

Now, at the mention of the prowlers, Bill said, "Don't worry about them. I'll handle it."

## WILD BILL TAKES AIM

David Reil didn't die. Not even close, contrary to Gary's prediction. The doctor determined David had suffered a concussion, but assured the Reils that the surface wounds and the internal damage would heal nicely with time. We were all relieved. The excitement of the night gave way to the routine of the new day. With one exception. Wild Bill announced at breakfast that he had some news.

Having gotten up with the sunrise, Bill spotted footprints left behind by the attackers and tracked them back in the direction of the chicken coop. Bill was prepared to take countermeasures. He intended to stand watch that evening—with his .30-06 rifle. I got the impression that he was a shoot-first-ask-questions-later kind of guy. My brother Dave wasn't scheduled to work and offered to make the rounds with his tiny six-inch knife. That didn't seem particularly wise, but Dave wanted to help.

As Dave later relayed the story, he and Bill took up positions in the yard. According to Bill's plan, he'd sit in the chicken coop as the first line of defense. With a point, he directed Dave to stay in the brush near the house in case the prowlers sneaked across the ravine and approached from the rear.

Occasionally, they'd leave their posts and, under the moonlight, make the rounds. After a quick tour of the immediate property on foot, Bill heading to the left and Dave to the right, they'd return to their spots and wait. And wait some more.

Several hours passed without any sign of trouble. Still crouching behind the thicket, my brother started to rethink the wisdom of engaging some trespasser with his puny blade. Besides, was he really prepared to stab someone? To kill them maybe? The more he thought about it, the more he became convinced that confronting the prowlers was nuts.

Abandoning his post, Dave hiked over to the chicken coop, softly calling Bill's name as he approached. The last thing Dave wanted was to be mistaken for a bad guy and get shot. He found Bill holding his rifle like a sniper, scanning the yard from the wash to the house and back. He was all business, dead set on killing someone to avenge what was done to David Reil. He'd probably planned to toss the body—or bodies—into the ravine behind the house. For several minutes, neither man spoke as Wild Bill, with his hand on the trigger, scanned, searching for the enemy.

Evidently, about the moment my brother Dave was going to tell Bill to call the whole thing off, I came bounding out the front door looking for Dave. At the sudden sound, Bill wheeled his gun around to shoot me. Acting on impulse, Dave part-grabbed and part-knocked the gun up into the air before Bill could get off a shot. No question, if Dave hadn't been there, I would have been wounded, if not killed.

Back safely inside the house, my brother told me how close I'd come to taking a bullet. I couldn't believe what I was hearing. I mean, I was thankful that Dave had rescued me. And yet, I'd recently been accused of attempted murder ... and now *I* had almost been murdered.

Closing my eyes that night, I felt utterly alone. At no point did I ever feel integrated into the Reils' family. At best, we were two families—make that three, counting Wild Bill—living in one house rather than one big happy family. Everyone had to fend for themselves. There was no love or kindness or tenderness displayed toward us. Not to mention I was never fully trusted by Mr. Reil.

I'll be the first to admit it was gracious of the Reils to take us in. I'm sure they originally wanted to help us out of a jam. But that noble motive was quickly tainted by the money they received through the social security survivor benefits from my mom. We never saw a penny; they never bought us anything to wear. We didn't receive presents at Christmas, and, for the most part, we were made to feel very much on the outside.

I wondered how living with my dad could be any worse.

In some ways, living with the Reils on the western edge of the Mojave Desert was a fitting metaphor for my life. The Mojave Desert is the location of Death Valley—a place where those who lose their way have no hope. That's exactly how I felt in my soul. At 282 feet below sea level, the Mojave Desert is the lowest point in North America. I was at the lowest point in my life. I felt utterly alone, abandoned, anxious.

Powerful feelings of loneliness had a way of overwhelming me at the most inconvenient times, like while I was sitting in my fourth- and fifth-grade class at Morongo Valley Elementary School. On several occasions as I listened to my teacher, Mr. Todd, a wave of sadness would broadside me. Tears would burn at the edges of my eyes. I'd literally get up in the middle of the lesson and walk outside, sit on the sandy hill at the edge of the school property, and just cry.

You know, I always sensed that God met me there. While I didn't have a Christian experience until I was fifteen, I'd sit on the hill and say, "God, where are you? Where's my dad? Why did Mom have to die? Will I always have to live with the Reils? Why does my life have to be like this?" The answers didn't have to come—just pouring out my heart to God seemed to keep the burden from crushing me.

At times the school nurse, Mrs. Bandy, would join me. She'd take a seat next to me and slip her arm around my shoulders. She usually wouldn't say anything more than, "It'll be okay, Jimmy. Hang in there, kiddo." *But Mrs. Bandy, you don't know the Reils!* I thought. Gary hit on me. David married his cousin. Marky stole my things and called me a liar. Mr. Reil thought I was trying to kill him. And the prowlers haunted us at night.

How would everything be okay?

One particular afternoon after these events had taken place, Mrs. Bandy sat down and handed me a Kleenex and some amazing news. She said, "I have a message from your brother."

"Dave?"

"No, from Mike. He's coming to visit you tomorrow."

8

# Dad: Take 2

Sleep was out of the question … *Mike was coming!*

I hadn't seen my brother in a hundred years. Okay, so it was more like four months, but the time apart might as well have been a century. I wouldn't be more excited if the Lone Ranger himself rode into town on the back of his white horse to rescue me.

The only news that might top this would be to learn my dad was with him. Mike and my dad had their share of conflicts, but were alike in a number of ways. Same height. Same facial features. Similar mannerisms. Athletic. A visit with Mike would be like having my dad drop by … almost.

With Mike in town, I knew I'd have an escape from my crazy, mixed-up life—at least for a few wonderful hours. Like sunshine after a long, cold Alaskan winter, I could feel a part of myself thawing, that part of me I'd locked safely away in a deep freeze to preserve. The funny, playful, expressive side of me didn't seem to fit into the Reils' *unusual* world.

When Mike sailed into town, he was tanned and brawny, his hair clipped as short as a bristle brush. He was full of tales from the high seas. He spoke of a jungle called Vietnam on the other side of the world, of war protesters in tie-dyed shirts, beads, and bell-bottoms, and of a man on his ship who introduced him to something called Christianity. While Mike didn't go into details, I got the impression that whatever Christianity was, Mike still had his doubts.

Being with him, I felt safe. Mike was an entire navy battle group of hope pulling into port. To me, the Reils lacked a vision or even the desire to rise above infighting and pettiness. By contrast, Mike inspired confidence. He represented strength, bravery, and a man on a mission. I'd sail anywhere, face any storm, with Mike as my captain at the helm.

Although just twenty years old, Mike was perceptive. His military training conditioned him to be particularly discerning. Even though his visit was brief, he quickly detected the friction in the house. The tension at the Reils was as thick as a handmade milkshake. What he saw concerned him. He could tell the Reils were sending us a message. Their actions made it clear we were not a part of their family, that our welcome was wearing off, and perhaps we ought to be leaving.

Finding us a different home, while important, wasn't Mike's top priority. Rather, he wanted to know how I was dealing with the living arrangements, with school, with my feelings about Mom. We'd go for walks, hang out, and just talk. Guy talk. Throughout the day, Mike pursued my heart. He'd ask, "Jimmy, how are you doing?" and, "Are you sure you're okay?" This probing didn't feel like the inquiry of a school official, or the impersonal cross-examination by a social worker. We spoke brother to brother. You know how that made me feel?

Loved.

Mike didn't have to bring me gifts, new clothes, or a treat. This big navy man—who'd faced far more serious battles than our ongoing skirmishes at the Reils'—cared about my well-being, and that was enough. Sure, he was visibly upset that Marky was a thief, that Mr. Reil was going senile, and that we lived in such primitive conditions. Who, in their right mind, wouldn't be? But most importantly, he *cared* about *me*. His unconditional love put fresh wind in my sails.

What's more, Mike had a news flash of his own. He pulled Dave, Dee Dee, and I together to tell us that he'd been in contact with Dad—more accurately, that Dad had been searching for us. Unbelievable! I was floored. I couldn't get over the fact that my dad had been looking for us. Not with a hammer, bent on revenge, but out of a desire to find us—to find me. The wave of euphoria I felt just about knocked me over.

We ambushed Mike with rapid-fire questions: Where was Dad living? How was he doing? Did he know Mom had died? Was there any chance he'd come and visit us? What about us going to see him? At one point Mike and Dave ended up in a heated exchange over the most obvious question: Could we go and live with Dad? Anything had to be better than our current circumstances, or so Dave believed. But Mike didn't think the idea of handing us off to Dad was wise.

Not yet. Maybe never.

But what about a visit? Mike wasn't sure Dad could handle three of us descending on him all at once. Evidently, he was emotionally fragile and not doing particularly well after learning about Mom's death. By the time we'd finished discussing the pros and cons of a family reunion, Mike agreed that a few days spent with Dad would probably be a good thing, especially for me. In the end, everyone agreed I should be the one to go. But how? Dave graciously offered to pay for my bus fare. Since Mike was heading back to sea, Dave would also make the arrangements.

To me, that was Christmas in October.

Dinner rolled around much too quickly for my tastes. Sitting elbow-to-elbow with Mike, I ate slowly as if that would delay the inevitable. I knew that when we finished, Mike would return to his ship. I must have chewed each bite ten times. I almost choked at the thought of his leaving. Mike was a bridge to memories of better times, when Mom was alive, and we were a family living in our own home. Soon his chair would be empty, and I felt the sadness gnawing away at the edges of my heart.

I had to laugh, though, at the look on Mike's face when he learned what we were eating for dinner. At 6'5" and 300 pounds of muscle, Mike could pack away the food. He'd been lifting weights and needed his protein. Licking his fingers, he said, "This is the *best* beef I've ever had. They sure don't cook like this on the ship."

Marky smirked. "Beef? Where'd you get that idea? That ain't beef."

"Really?" Mike said, skewering another piece. "Could have fooled me. What is it?"

Gary said, "Remember that burro that knocked you off its back?"

Mike nodded, his mouth full of "beef." The last time Mike had come to visit, he thought it would be great fun to catch a ride on a donkey the Reils had in the yard. The donkey, however, didn't take too kindly to Mike's girth on its back. Mike was as startled as the rest of us when the donkey took off running, dumping him in the bushes. Picking the briers from his skin, he had no shortage of choice words for that "hideous creature."

Mike chewed a little slower, then swallowed. "Yeah, what happened to that thing anyway?"

Marky said, "That's what you're eating!"

The look on Mike's face was priceless.

## HOMEWARD BOUND

When I lived at the Reils', there was this thought I'd carry around with me, much like a kid who refuses to give up his tattered Linus blanket. I always thought I'd find my dad, that he'd be glad to see me, that we'd live together, and maybe, just maybe, we'd feel like a family once again. Now that Dad had made contact with Mike, and plans were set in motion for me to go see him, I was several steps closer to realizing my dream.

Mike must have read my mind. Before he left, he made a point of warning me that Dad "still had his issues." I know he was trying to protect me from getting my hopes up only to have them dashed against the hard reality of his addictions. He might have thought that I was too young to remember Dad's history of bad choices with gambling and alcohol and his difficulty keeping promises—as if I'd forgotten about the mitt Dad promised to bring me.

Time has a way of reconstructing history, either for better or worse. Mike probably assumed I was glossing over the past with rose-colored glasses. I wasn't. I just liked to focus on my dad's positive qualities. I preferred to dwell on those things about him that I admired. Still, I knew he had problems and a few eccentric ideas, not in a Mr. Reil sleeping-in-the-rabbit-hutch sort of way. He was more of a *frustrated perfectionist*.

When I was four, for example, back when we were living on Cosby Street, I recall that my dad got really, really mad with the city trash collector. Back then, most everybody had those forty-four-gallon aluminum trash cans with the corrugated ridges on the sides. I'm not sure what ticked him off. Maybe the garbagemen didn't put the lids back on after emptying the cans, in which case the lids would blow down the street or get flattened by a passing car. Perhaps the guys dented the sides of the can against the back of the trash truck, or left pieces of litter on the sidewalk. Whatever the infraction, they made Dad so mad he refused to pay for garbage pickup.

Instead of the regular Tuesday-Friday waste pickup, he wanted to prove he didn't need them and their lousy service. His plan? He closed and locked the front of our garage door. For a solid year, we packed the garage—from floor to ceiling, wall to wall, and front to back—with garbage. How was I to know that sort of thing was abnormal? My dad said to put the trash in the garage, so we did.

Keep in mind that the weather in Southern California never really cools down. Year-round the temperatures tend to hover in the seventies. With the sun roasting the air like a solar microwave, our garage became like a giant version of an Easy Bake Oven. Between the decaying trash and the worms who, I'm sure, were enjoying themselves entirely too much, our garage became the world's largest compost box.

One night after discovering he couldn't shove any more trash through the back door, Dad announced, "I'm going to get a trailer." He didn't mind hauling the filth to the dump; he was too pleased with himself that he didn't need "that stinking trashman." Looking back, I'd have to say there are better ways to make your point.

Like I said, I tended to be forgiving of such flaws while embracing his strengths. For example, I have fond memories of the way he'd make breakfast on Sunday to let my mom get some rest. After lunch, he'd take us for a Sunday-afternoon drive to places like the Joshua Tree National Monument where we'd climb rocks, scuff our knees, and enjoy each other's company.

Dad was particularly sensitive to Mom's need for rest. We owned a 1957 Chevy station wagon, and he placed a mattress in the back so Mom could sleep during those long drives. We'd get home and Dad would fire up the grill. He was, in my mind, the most fantastic barbeque chef in the world. Which is why, among other reasons, I was just about jumping out of my skin to see him for the weekend.

I ducked out of school early that glorious Friday, just after lunch, to catch the bus. Dave sat with me on the bench at the bus stop until the red, white, and blue Greyhound rumbled into view. The behemoth, a forty-foot MCI-M7, stopped at the curb with a blast of its air brakes and a belch of diesel. Its tires were almost as tall as me. The shiny chrome door swung outward, and the driver, wearing sunglasses, a blue shirt, and holding a cup of coffee, emerged. He took a final sip, tossed the empty container in a garbage can, and called out the destination.

I hugged Dave, and boarded clutching my ticket and my knapsack, taking a window seat toward the back. I sat up so high I could see the other end of the world. I could even see the driver's bald spot on the top of his head as he inspected the tires beneath me. As it turned out, I was the only passenger departing from that station. With just one ticket to collect and no luggage to stow, the driver had us rolling down the road within a few short minutes. I leaned against the window for a final wave good-bye. I felt like a grown-up, taking a trip by myself—at only age ten.

Aside from the yellow Blue Bird buses used by my public school, I'd never been on a *real* bus, one with carpet and cloth seats that reclined. Acquainting myself with my surroundings, I counted forty-three seats and nine other passengers. There were three other kids on the bus; I was the only one without an adult. I had hoped there'd be a bathroom. Dave said some buses had them. No such luck. I'd have to hold it.

The trip to San Gabriel would take several hours, but I didn't care. I was finally going to see my dad. When we passed by the Palm Springs exit twenty minutes later, I knew I wasn't dreaming. I was really on the road. I yearned for the chance to be "normal" for a few days and to sleep without fear of the prowlers. I still struggled with memories of the face in the window.

But, most of all, I couldn't wait to eat regular food.

Because the Reils were on welfare (although they did receive Mr.

Reil's disability payment and our foster-care check), and in light of the fact that there were so many mouths to feed, they'd shop in volume at an army surplus store. Once every couple of weeks, they'd come home with five-pound blocks of cheese, bins of butter, cases of noodles, sacks filled with instant hot chocolate mix, and peanut butter by the gallon. These staples would supplement what was grown and killed on their property.

Nothing against donkey meat, but a genuine hamburger and a milkshake sounded really nice.

I hadn't had a shake or ice cream in eight months—back when my mom was still alive. What I wouldn't give to have something other than hot chocolate and cinnamon toast for breakfast. Maybe eggs the way Dad used to serve them, sunny-side up, with a side of bacon, and toast with peanut butter and jelly on it. I could picture Dad serving my plate, the steam rising like a smoke signal telling me that breakfast was ready.

With visions of milkshakes and eggs on my mind, I rocked in my seat as if that would help the bus roll down the road faster. When that failed to make a noticeable difference, I slid to the aisle seat where I could see the bus driver in his mirror. Maybe he'd notice how anxious I was to get to San Gabriel and step on the pedal.

## REACH OUT AND TOUCH SOMEONE

I got to my new seat just in time to watch a bit of drama unfold up ahead. A man wearing a weathered tan hat with a floppy brim—the kind worn by fishermen—and a wrinkled windbreaker started talking to one of the other kids on the bus. The boy wasn't much older than I was. He sat across the aisle from the hatted stranger.

I assumed the man was a stranger because the boy's father glared at him. Raising a hand as if to say, "No problem, I'll move," the hatted stranger rose and made his way toward the rear, gripping the top of the seat backs as he walked.

He stopped midway down the aisle as if momentarily disoriented, or perhaps to scan the faces, then continued. With a half smile, he took the seat directly across the aisle from me. He slumped back into his seat, removed his hat, and dabbed his forehead with a handkerchief. He rolled his head in my direction, placed his hat on his lap, and started to make small talk.

"So, what's your name, kid?"

"Jimmy."

"Nice name. Jimmy. I got a friend named Jimmy. Yeah, that's a real nice name. Sure is."

I turned to look out the window on my side of the bus when he nudged my arm.

"Is this your first bus ride, Jimmy?"

"Yes."

"Where'd you say you were going?"

"I didn't. I'm going to see my dad."

"That should be fun. And your mom, too?"

"No … she's dead."

His eyebrows narrowed. He reached over and squeezed my arm. "Gee, Jimmy. That's a tough break. Sure is." He fell silent for a moment, then added, "Um, you know what? My mother's dead too."

"Really?"

"Yeah … I know how you must feel, Jimmy." He started gently tapping my forearm. I offered a smile, unsure what to say. He looked over his shoulder and then back at me.

"So … does that mean you're traveling alone?"

I nodded.

A wide smile eased across his face. "Really? Me, too. Isn't that something? We guys should stick together, right?"

Another nod. Another silence.

I really wasn't trying to be rude. I just didn't feel like talking. I had too many thoughts in my head about seeing Dad. You know, would he be as glad to see me as I was to see him? Would he hug me? Would he look the same? Where did he live? Work? Would there be time to play catch? Should I hug him if he didn't hug me? Would he make his famous Saturday-morning breakfast?

"Care for a LifeSaver, Jimmy?" the hat man said, interrupting my thoughts. He popped a candy in his mouth and then peeled back the multicolor wrapper. He extended the treat toward me. "Go ahead, have one."

"That's great, thanks."

I plucked one from the pack. He said, "You know something, Jimmy?"

I handed back the LifeSavers. "What?"

"Well, I was kind of wondering if you'd do me a little favor."

"What's that?"

"Do you mind if I … if I held your hand?"

"Huh?"

"You know, Jimmy, like friends do. I'd like that."

He seemed nice enough. He sounded as if he were alone in the world, like my dad. What did I know? At least I couldn't see the harm in his request. Keep in mind I didn't have anyone coaching me about the prospects of meeting a pedophile on the bus. I had no idea what that was, just as I didn't understand why Gary would tell me I was cute.

"I guess that's okay," I said.

The man's eyes widened as he reached over and took my hand in his. I figured he was glad for the company. The bus driver, however, figured something different. He was watching this action unfold in his mirror. Evidently, the driver had his suspicions about this guy.

Without warning, I felt the bus start to brake and veer to the right. That was odd. We weren't getting off at an exit. Maybe we had a flat tire? Did buses with those huge tires get flats?

The driver pulled the bus onto the shoulder of the highway, opened the door, and then worked his way toward us. His sunglasses were off. So were his gloves. The hat man dropped my hand as if I were suddenly infected with a contagious disease. The driver pointed to the man, all businesslike.

"I don't know what you're into, pal, but you need to get off of my bus. Now."

"Hey—hold on. We were just having a little friendly conversation, right, Jimmy?"

"Leave the kid out of this," the driver said, folding his arms. "Get your things and get moving before I throw you off."

"But what about my ticket? I paid to go—"

The driver cut him off. "Sorry, pal, this is the end of the road for you."

We left the hat man with his luggage by the side of the road and then drove off. *What did he do?* I thought. I'd learn later in life about the significance of what had happened. The Greyhound driver, however, knew full well what was going on, and put the brakes to it. Thanks to him, I dodged another bullet.

## HOME RUNS, HOT DOGS, AND PLEDGES OF ALLEGIANCE

The bus driver encouraged me to take a seat closer to the front, which was fine with me; this way I could see the bugs colliding with the windshield. Before I knew it, we were pulling into the Greyhound terminal. Dad planned to meet me at the loading dock. I figured picking him out of the crowd would be easy since he was so tall. I was almost shaking with anticipation.

A moment later, we parked at the curb. The brakes exhaled with a gush of air, as if they'd been holding their breath for the last two hours, and the door opened with a *whoosh*. The driver descended down the stairs with me riding his heels. I saw Dad waiting by the boarding gate; when he saw me, his smile almost didn't fit on his face.

We hugged forever—and yet it wasn't long enough.

Since Dad didn't own a car, we boarded a local transit bus for the trip to his place. I can't recall the details of what we spoke about during the brief commute, but it didn't matter. I was with my dad and for those unforgettable moments that was all I needed. I sat straight and proud and as close to him as the seats allowed. Nobody could pull us apart.

Dad lived in a modest, one-bedroom flat in San Gabriel. Probably the most unexpected thing I remember about his apartment was the plastic furniture. The white chairs with stick arms and legs and matching table sort of resembled an outdoor patio set—definitely a far cry from the table and chairs we owned as a family when Dad worked at a furniture factory.

While he hadn't draped a Welcome Home sign above the apartment door, he shocked me when he handed me a brand-new baseball and asked if I wanted to get a Dodger Dog. What? Was he serious? Go see the Los Angeles Dodgers vs. the Cincinnati Reds ... in a doubleheader? Best of all, if we got there in time, we might get my ball autographed. I floated. I was going to my first major league baseball game—with Dad. Mike and Dave would be so jealous.

Dad told me to toss my stuff in the bedroom and wash up. We'd have to hurry to catch the bus to Dodger Stadium. Minutes later, we ran to the bus stop, but the taillights of our bus could be seen moving away just as we arrived. Dad tried to assure me another bus would come along soon enough, but I was brokenhearted. I kept saying, "We're *never* going to get there in time."

My dad, seeing the disappointment, flagged down a cab. I knew that was a big sacrifice on his part; Dad disliked paying taxi fare the same way he disliked paying for our trash service back on Cosby Street. The trip from San Gabriel to Los Angeles was upward of thirty miles. Thanks to some fancy Friday-night driving, we arrived a half an hour before the game with enough time to meet some of the players.

I smiled so wide my face could barely contain it. My baseball had been signed by Johnny Bench, Steve Garvey, Joe Morgan, Pete Rose, and Davey Lopes. Best of all, I was with my dad. For hours I cheered until my voice was hoarse, downed Dodger Dogs and Orange Crush soda, and, for the first time in years, felt like a kid again.

Here's the funny thing about that ball. Weeks later, a bunch of guys from school wanted to play baseball at lunch. One problem. We didn't have a ball. Remembering my autographed treasure, which, amazingly, Marky didn't steal, I brought the autographed ball to school. Needless to say, by the end of recess my shiny white ball was black; the merciless asphalt pavement had taken off all the signatures, too. That ball would probably be worth a few hundred dollars today.

After the Dodgers game, we caught the last bus to San Gabriel. With a full heart and the rhythm of the wheels humming against the pavement, I fell asleep on my dad's lap. Saturday morning, the smell of bacon and eggs enticed me out from under the covers. I went to the kitchen and found my dad working his magic at the stove as if he were auditioning for Emeril's cooking show. A towel hung from his shoulder as he put the finishing touches on our plates.

I rubbed the sleep from my eyes and took a seat. I was afraid to blink for fear that when my eyes reopened, he'd be gone and I'd be back at the Reils'. Within a moment, he joined me and served us the best sunny-side up eggs this side of heaven. He hadn't lost his touch.

As we ate, we talked about the Dodger game. Dad was such a big fan with no shortage of opinions on what our manager might have done differently—maybe start a lefty against their righty. Stuff like that. He asked me how I was doing at school and at the Reils'. But, as I answered, I secretly hoped Dad would get around to asking me the big question, the one I'd been longing to answer:

*Jimmy, do you want to live with me?*

I'd privately rehearsed the answer in my head for months.

*I wouldn't be any trouble....*

*I'd be happy to sleep on the floor....*

*I'd eat anything—well, preferably not donkey....*

*I could even do a few chores. Just ask me the question, Dad. Please ask me to stay.*

Dad fell silent for a minute, as if deep in thought. When he finished eating, he wiped the edge of his mouth with his napkin. When he cleared his throat to speak, my heart jumped.

"Jimmy, would you like seconds?"

# 9

# Great Expectations

**M**y eyes were pinched shut. I inhaled a deep, searching breath. Nothing. I filled my lungs again. Still nothing. I was lying on my cot at the Reils' trying to detect a trace of my father's scent lingering on my clothing from his hug good-bye. His unique blend of Old Spice covering the tracks of lime-scented Gillette Foamy had taken up residence on my shirt and stayed there for hours.

I breathed in, but the fragrance had vanished. Even the details of his face seemed to fade from remembrance far too quickly; almost with the speed of a sweet dream I wanted to remember but couldn't recall when I blinked awake. I wanted to remember and so I kept my eyes pinned tight; I refused to let go of my memories of the time spent with Dad.

I had returned to the depressing land of headless chickens, donkey meat, Wild Bill, prowlers, and vats of hot chocolate, but I didn't immediately acknowledge that reality. I lay motionless in my cocoon, a reluctant butterfly dreaming of the day I'd break free of that place.

My dad never got around to asking me to live with him during that otherwise great weekend. I'm not sure why, but he didn't bring the idea up on his own and I wasn't entirely comfortable inviting myself into his world. I certainly didn't want to say anything that might cause him to regret inviting me or jeopardize the prospects of future visits. Most of all, I didn't want him to disappear from my life again.

Sure, I was disappointed. I had a dad-shaped hole in my heart like every other boy on the planet. I yearned for him to play sports with me and take me hunting and fishing. I wanted to learn how to pound crooked nails into scraps of wood, build a rocket ship to the moon, and design the best go-cart on this side of the planet.

I wanted to know my dad would be there to show me the ropes as I got older. I needed him to show me how to shave once the peach fuzz on my chin demanded a real razor, and tell me how to ask a girl for a date without my voice cracking. I needed him to prepare me for the Round Table of manhood, where I might one day fight with the bravest of knights to win the hand of a beautiful maiden.

Most of all, I needed someone who believed in me.

True, I had a male figure in my life—Mr. Reil. But he wasn't the mentoring type, and I had difficulty picturing King Arthur inviting him into the fellowship of the knights. While Mr. Reil had plenty of opportunities to be a mentor, he never took the initiative. Even with all of the cars scattered around his property in need of repair, he never took the time to introduce me to a socket wrench. He didn't show me how to change the oil, or a flat, or even an air filter.

Yes, I did get a lesson in chicken chopping, but knowing my way around a car would have been of more long-term value than knowing how to decapitate a bird—unless, of course, I was contemplating a career in heavy metal music.

If the roles had been reversed and I were the dad, I know I would have asked my son to come and live with me in a heartbeat. And why not? We were family. Though I needed a mentor, and wanted my dad, I wasn't entirely surprised that he hadn't reached across the table and, with a squeeze to the back of my neck, said, "Jimmy, how soon can you move in with your old man?" Like I said, I was disappointed, but not crushed. I might have been young, but I was well on my way to developing a personal philosophy of life, for lack of a better phrase. The first principle life taught me went like this: *Keep your expectations low. That way you don't get hurt.*

The seeds of that viewpoint had been sown back when my dad didn't bring me the baseball mitt he promised. The roots were watered when I met Larry of the Three Stooges, who didn't turn out to be the funny, crazy person I expected, like the guy on television. When Hank the Tank rolled into our family with a mission to love my mom without targeting any of his love toward us, the seedlings of low expectations put down deep roots.

When nobody in my life prepared me for the death of my mother, when the Reils sided with Marky and suggested I was the troublemaker, when Mr. Reil accused me of attempting to kill him, and—the hardest hurt of all—when my own dad didn't want me to live with him, my emerging outlook on life helped me survive the impact. Keeping my expectations low was like strapping a bullet-proof vest around my spirit.

Although I had no control over my circumstances, I could control my response. I had low expectations, but I never crossed over to pessimism. I believed that something better was waiting around the corner; my life and my circumstances *would* improve if I plowed ahead and stayed focused on doing my best with what I had. I also couldn't shake the sense that God was somehow there with me, just as Grandpa Hope had said God was with my mom when she died. I didn't know how it all worked, but God must have known the hunger of my heart and given me the strength to move forward.

ONCE UPON A DREAM

A remarkable turn of events occurred about four months after I returned to Morongo Valley from seeing my dad, and not a moment too soon. The tension at the Reils' was incredibly thick. Not a good thick, like the middle of an Oreo Double Stuff cookie. More like a destructive thick, like a hot lava flow inflaming everything it touched. Mr. Reil continued to lose touch with reality as dementia started to set in, which, I later learned, is why he viewed me as Public Enemy Number One. Naturally, Mrs. Reil felt the need to protect her family's well-being and was quick to favor her kids over us.

I stopped talking around them since anything I said seemed to fuel the paranoia. I drank my watery hot chocolate and ate my chewy cinnamon toast in silence. I went to school where at least nobody thought I was plotting to push them off of a cliff. In fact, my athletic ability even gained me respect on the playground. Then I'd return to the Reils' where I took cover by being as invisible as I could. I'd play outside, out of sight until dinner, ate without daring to ask Mr. Reil to pass the salt, and went to bed early, where I watched spiders and moths and wondered if the prowlers might return.

When school let out for the summer, I spent the day exploring the outdoors, looking for soda bottles to return for a little spending money, and generally kept clear of the Reils. Never once did they suggest that I invite anyone from my fifth-grade class over to play. And rather than create more friction, I didn't ask. As I hiked, stick in hand, I held on to the hope that something good was around the corner.

There just had to be.

One particularly hot mid-August Friday night, I had already switched off the light and fallen asleep when I heard Dave come home late from work. He sat on the edge of his adjacent cot, and the springs bearing his weight protested. A raspy series of squeaks simultaneously announced his arrival and pulled me out of my sleep. Dave poked my side.

"Pssst! Jimmy. You awake?"

"Hmm?"

"Guess what?" Dave said, just above a whisper.

I rolled over on my side, blinked my eyes open with a yawn. "Um, is Mr. Reil sleeping with the rabbits again?"

"No, silly...."

"Hold on, what time is it?"

"Midnight. But, listen, Jimmy, Dad's coming!"

I scratched my head while his statement made its way through my ear canal, and across a network of semi-alert electrodes to the corner of my brain trying to process this information. The fog in my head lifted a notch.

"Dad? As in our dad?"

"Isn't that great?"

I was understandably suspicious of anything that resembled good news, especially when offered in the dead of night. After all, good news was about as rare as scrambled eggs at breakfast—we just didn't get it.

"You're serious?" I said, a little too loudly. Marky stirred, but kept on snoring.

"Serious as a heart attack," Dave said in hushed tones. Not wanting to share the glorious news with Marky or Gary—at least not yet—I matched Dave's volume.

"How do you know?"

"He called. He's really coming, Jimmy."

"When?"

"Tomorrow. Probably around lunch."

With the fog now lifted, I tried to envision Dad eating lunch at the kitchen table with the Reils.

"I can't believe it. Dad's really coming ... here?"

"Would I joke about something like that?"

For a moment, I was conflicted. I wanted to believe Dave. But would this turn out to be another one of my dad's broken promises? A twinge of doubt surfaced in my heart, tethering the wings of hope back to reality. I laid down and stared at the gray ceiling; my feet wiggled left to right under the covers as I tried to process the conflicting emotions.

"But how? Dad doesn't even have a car."

Dave didn't answer at first. I turned and saw, even in the darkness, a glint of white as his smile widened. My eyes narrowed in expectation. I got the impression Dave was withholding something.

"Mike's bringing him." The words hung in the air.

"*Mike? For real?*"

"Ha! Can you believe it?!"

If I hadn't already been sitting down, I think I would have fallen over. Instead, I fell back against my pillow and floated somewhere over the moon. *Dad and Mike were coming. Here. Tomorrow.* Having dropped this bombshell, Dave gave me a quiet high five before leaving to take a shower.

Sleep was impossible. I lay awake with a few million thoughts. *Why was Dad coming? Just a friendly visit? Had Mike told Dad how difficult life was for us? Was Dad coming to rescue me from the Reils? This time, would he ask that question: Do you want to live with me? If he did, I'd answer him with the biggest bear hug in the world.*

The next morning I dressed quickly and then skipped breakfast, which, to Mr. Reil, was probably a sign that I was planning some sort of mutiny. Rather than try and explain anything, I headed to the front of the property to hang out by the chicken coop. Dad was coming and I'd be waiting. The chickens, however, deserved to know that I came in peace. I explained that I wasn't there to wield the ax, just to pass the time.

They appeared to appreciate that.

I kicked rocks, searched for lizards, and waited. The empty dirt road on the other side of the wash beckoned, and for a minute I contemplated hiking down those dusty miles to wait by the mailboxes. That way I could spot the first signs of Mike's yellow and white '57 Chevy on the horizon. But Dave said they wouldn't arrive until lunch, so I decided to stay put. At least hanging by the henhouse provided some level of interest: I could watch the chickens peck away at the ground in their endless search for the perfect bug-meal—it was sort of like watching a special on the Discovery Channel today.

When the chicken-watching grew old, I scratched the backs of the rabbits right behind their floppy ears, which I knew they loved. If, on the off chance my dad asked me to live with him, I knew I'd miss the animals. Maybe I felt a certain affinity for their plight considering we were both trapped in a cage of sorts, longing to be free. Spending a little extra time that morning seemed an appropriate way to say good-bye—just in case.

## SAY THE WORD

There's a world of difference between having a roof over your head at night and being at home. Staying at a hotel, while providing shelter, just isn't home. The pillows are harder. The towels feel as if they've been dipped in industrial laundry soap that washed away their original softness. The pictures on the wall, with their pastel splatters, seem mechanically designed by a computer program to maximize the color coordination with the drapes.

Life at the Reils' never felt like home to me. Sure, I was thankful for a roof over my head, a place to bathe, and food to eat. But I never felt settled. I certainly didn't feel loved. I didn't even have the freedom to wander into the kitchen and help myself to a snack. I couldn't ask to have the patio room where we slept painted something other than warehouse gray. I couldn't hang a portrait of my mother on the wall, even if I'd had one. I was increasingly aware that the management viewed my siblings and me as undesirable guests and was counting the minutes until checkout time.

The feelings were mutual. I wanted to get out of the Reils' almost from the moment we drove up to their flamingo-pink house. Maybe when Dad arrived, he'd pick up on the negative undercurrent flowing through the place and decide to break me out. Dave and Dee Dee, knowing I held such hopes, kept telling me that my dad wasn't a stable guy. Living with him might not be such a good alternative.

Whenever they'd make that point, I'd think, *How could Dad be any less stable than Mr. Reil?* I didn't feel like I was trying to pick between two bad choices. Living with Dad was a good option. In my heart I knew it was the *best* option—if only he'd say those magical words I longed to hear.

Just before noon, I heard tires crunching gravel in the distance. Because of the dust that plumed overhead, I couldn't see the vehicle until it almost reached the wash, but I could tell the car was close by. When Mike's '57 Chevy appeared, I jumped up and down, waving my arms as if directing a jet across the tarmac.

As promised, my dad came.

He really came.

The euphoria of being found, of being with Dad again, was

almost too much for me to handle. My heart pounded so hard I was sure Dad could hear it. Even with all of "that stuff" that my siblings said he had struggled with, I couldn't have been happier to see him. Grinning ear to ear, Mike hit the horn as they rode down and then up the other side of the wash as if it were opening day at Disneyland and they were riding the Matterhorn.

While I was still waving my arms like a rooster, Mike tapped the horn and pulled the car toward the house. I chased after them like a tailwind, a clutch of chickens following in my wake. Within seconds, Dee Dee and Dave bounded out the front door of the house and surrounded the car as if royalty had arrived. Mike cut the engine and Dad emerged.

Dad wore a bright orange shirt, chocolate brown slacks, and a light tan jacket. His hair seemed a tad grayer, but his smile was as wide and as grand as the canyon. He was still in good shape. As I hugged my dad, I inhaled deeply as if that would help me memorize his scent. If only I could somehow bottle it. With the exception of Kim, who had married and moved away, we were a family once again.

It felt good. I felt whole.

At Dad's suggestion, we piled into the car and drove to town to have lunch together. I wouldn't be surprised if Mike had a hand in promoting that idea, considering the donkey meat he was served during his last visit. Come to think of it, we were so swept away by the reunion, we didn't think to introduce Dad to the Reils until after we returned.

We hadn't been together since well before my mom had died, and the three hours of laughing, swapping stories, and catching up flew by far too quickly. The main question running through my mind was, *Is Dad gonna ask me to stay with him?* As the afternoon drifted toward evening, and nobody had raised that "big question,"

I started to feel a sense of urgency. I was determined to bring it up even if nobody else did. I wasn't going to let the chance pass me by.

Not this time.

The sun started its slow descent, and we gathered by Mike's car for a photo. As Mrs. Reil prepared to snap the picture, I could feel my father's hand resting on my right shoulder. The warmth of his body at my back as he stood behind me was more comforting than a thousand blankets. And yet, even with my dad standing so close, my heart felt as if it were sinking right along with the setting sun. *Why didn't anybody talk about the one question that mattered? Had they privately decided among themselves that I'd be better off staying at the Reils' than with my dad? Didn't my vote count?*

After Mrs. Reil took the picture, she handed the camera back to Dee Dee and left us alone to say our good-byes. My dad fished a Pall Mall cigarette from his jacket. I watched his hands as they maneuvered through the familiar routine of lighting up. He struck the match and, behind the safety of a cupped hand, lit the end. Tossing the matchstick to the ground, and grinding it in the dirt with his shoe, he exhaled.

"So, Jimmy, I hear you don't like living at the Reils', is that right?" he said.

I glanced at Dave and Dee Dee. They obviously *had* talked about what I was feeling. I just hadn't noticed. I felt the edges of my ears start to tingle as if sunburned. The problem was I didn't know where my dad was headed with his question. If I said, "Dad, it's nuts," would he launch into a pep talk about being thankful for a roof over my head? Or, would he pop the question I had hoped he'd ask? I decided to be truthful.

"Dad, it's pretty crazy, that's for sure."

He took another slow drag. "The Reils seem nice enough to me...."

"That's because you don't have to *live* with them," I countered, looking at Dave and Dee Dee for backup. Dave started to say something, but Dad raised a hand and cut him off.

"Jimmy, if half of what I heard today is true, I can see why you'd feel that way," he said, referring to our lunchtime conversation when we'd brought Dad up to speed on the prowlers, the dismal breakfast menu, the stealing, the taunts by Marky, everything. "I'll tell you what. I've been thinking, and I've decided you and Dee Dee can come back and live with me if you'd like. How's that sound?"

"Wow! Really, Dad?" I hugged him until my arms hurt.

"Whoa, champ. A man's gotta breathe," he said, patting me on the back. I straightened, took a step back, and pointed toward the house.

"Should I go get my stuff?"

"Slow down a second, Jimmy," he said with a grin. "I'll get it worked out. We'll take care of it in the next week or two."

Those were the longest two weeks of my life, just waiting for the big day when Dad would return to take us away. After Dad left, I asked Dave why he wasn't moving too. He said he didn't feel right about walking away from the two jobs he was working—at least not yet. Plus, being older, he had developed a network of friends.

As I counted off the days, I thought that by leaving the Reils' bizarre world behind, my life would become "normal." I had some idea of what a normal family ought to be thanks to my mom. Even though she was dead, I carried with me those wonderful early childhood memories of what a family was and what a home ought to be like.

Now it was just Dad in charge.

How bad could that be?

10

# Take Me Out of the Ball Game

Dee Dee and I moved into Dad's apartment and, in many ways, living with him was a blessing. Having the man I loved back in my life would have been enough, but there were other immediate benefits. I didn't have to share one bedroom with five guys or compete with ten people over a single bathroom. I drank whole milk and ate eggs and bacon. I'd spend hours at the pool after school, diving for coins or swimming laps.

However, I was no longer five years old as I had been the last time we'd lived under the same roof. I was eleven going on twelve and much more cognizant of what was going on around me. During those first few weeks of being reunited with Dad, I got the distinct impression that he wanted to do right by us, which is why he rescued us from the Reils'. At the same time, I could tell Dad was a troubled, haunted man.

The root cause of his distress was never talked about. His generation didn't openly share their feelings, at least not with the kids. I guess he preferred to engage his personal battles somewhere deep in his spirit. There were several times when he'd lose the fight and then turn to alcohol to cope. In those moments, I had to remind myself to continue to keep my expectations low so I wouldn't get hurt.

Every Friday night Dad would watch boxing on television. Dad loved his boxing. Sometimes with a dishtowel over his shoulder, he'd watch from the kitchen while preparing a snack. Whether sitting in the room or making popcorn by the stove, he maintained a running commentary with the fight. *Hit him—come on, don't be a wimp. Knock his lights out! Hey, that's a low blow, Ref!* Stuff like that.

He'd yell at the tube, clench his hands into fists, and punch the air in front of him as if it were *his* heavyweight title on the line. Sometimes I sat by his side for hours, content to watch him shadow-boxing.

Saturday nights we ate hot dogs, pork and beans, and "black cows," that great combination of vanilla ice cream and root beer soda. Sundays, we never went to church, but Dad would make barbecue religiously, as if competing in the county cook-off.

While those treats with Dad were a highlight, his behavior wasn't always healthy, especially when the drinking got out of hand. His episodes really troubled me. I didn't like the person he became when he was drunk, and I hated the distance his behavior created between us. I still loved him, I just didn't *like* him at times—like the Saturday he decided to come to my Little League game.

I loved baseball. Still do. Back then, when I slipped my hand into my leather glove, I knew I was becoming a part of something larger than myself. I was a member of a team. We called ourselves the Mets and, with a win/loss record above .500, we were quite good. Whether or not there was a scheduled practice, I'd walk five blocks to the ball field where, for hours, I'd snag fly balls and practice hitting with the team or whoever showed up on a given day.

Whenever we had our games, I was about the only kid who didn't have his dad around to cheer for him. Of course, that didn't keep me from talking up my dad to the guys—you know, bragging about how he had coached Little League most of his life and could pound a ball over the center-field fence as effortlessly as Babe Ruth.

One particular evening our game was scheduled to be played on the nicest of three adjacent fields, the one with the manicured grass infield and overhead lighting. Those towering lights bathed the field in artificial shafts of sunlight, which made me feel nervous, as if we were actually in the big leagues being watched by millions on TV. Since I was the shortstop, and sometimes covered first or third base, I always felt the energy of the crowd cheering me on.

About the third inning, I was sitting in the dugout with my team, when I heard, then saw, my dad in the crowded stands with the other parents. He was intoxicated. I had been so proud of him and couldn't wait for the day he'd come to see me play—until that moment. He wasn't just drunk; he was loud and obnoxious.

At home, when my dad would shout at the TV during fights, I thought it was funny. Here, his behavior was embarrassing. Dad stood and criticized the calls the umpire was making. *Come on, Ump, are you blind or stupid? That ball was a strike. How about getting a new pair of glasses?* His words were slurred, and his inebriated protests were definitely over the top.

More than a few times, he began to launch into a ridiculous diatribe when the action on the field picked up. Thankfully, the crowd response drowned him out. I wanted the noise to continue so that his lone drunken voice couldn't be heard.

When "that crazy man" in the stands pointed toward us, people around me started asking, "Whose dad is that?" I pulled my cap down and plowed my cleats into the earth beneath the bench. If I dug fast enough, maybe I could carve a hole large enough to crawl into. I refused to acknowledge *that man* was my father. When I stepped into the batter's box, he blew my cover. He called out my name, adding, "Thaaat's my bouy!"

I was humiliated.

After the game, I avoided walking home with him. I hid my team information so he wouldn't know when I was scheduled to play again. I wish I could say that was the last time he drank excessively. It wasn't. He became severely drunk five or six other times during the year we lived together. While he never threatened me with physical harm as he had threatened my mom, my siblings were growing concerned about the wisdom of me continuing to live with him.

As I said at the outset, the first principle life had taught me thus far was to keep my expectations low so I wouldn't get hurt. Watching Dad's public misbehavior, however, demonstrated that my philosophy wasn't foolproof. I *was* hurt by my father's actions. Further, I'd soon be crushed again, this time by yet another man I'd come to admire.

## SCHOOL OF HARD KNOCKS

Living with Dad required a change in schools. From the moment I started to attend San Gabriel Elementary School as a sixth grader, I was in panic mode. Everything about the school was new to me. I had to transition from a friendly country school in Morongo Valley, to a rough, big-city school in East Los Angeles. I was a new kid who didn't know anybody or anything about the system.

I didn't have just one teacher who covered all of the subjects. Instead, I had homeroom and a confusing array of teachers who taught different periods that required me to change classrooms several times during the day—all before the bell rang. I dreaded being assigned a locker with a built-in combination. What if I forgot the code? What if I couldn't get my books out fast enough to find the right room before the bell sounded?

Talk about pressure.

Thankfully, my homeroom teacher, Mr. Freid, was kind and, in many ways, a mentor to me. Mr. Freid was a reserve deputy sheriff for the city and taught karate as a fifth-degree black belt instructor. Everything about him—his manner of speaking, his stance, and the way he patrolled around the halls—exuded power. He was what every boy thought a man should be. I know I did.

When Mr. Freid suggested that I take his karate class, I felt like somebody cared. For six months I studied the Japanese art of karate under Mr. Freid. I was fascinated by the pressure-sensitive points on the body of an opponent where a well-placed kick or blow would neutralize him.

The highlight of our class was when Mr. Freid announced a special guest, Chuck Norris. We already thought a gung-ho guy like Mr. Freid with his police badge and black belt was invincible. But to discover he was also friends with famous people like Chuck Norris—*the* Chuck Norris who fought Bruce Lee in the then-popular movie *Way of the Dragon*—was incredible. Watching them spar on the mat was enough to convince me that my homeroom teacher was a rock.

Mr. Norris was invited, in part, to speak with us about the dangers of drugs and alcohol. The part of Mr. Norris's story that especially resonated with me had to do with his background. He was the son of an alcoholic. So was I. He talked about how his dad missed so much of his childhood. I knew the feeling. His mother was half Irish and half Indian—just like my mom. And yet, while his childhood sounded about as daunting as my own, he'd managed to rise above the challenges he'd faced to become a world-class competitor.

I was captivated as Mr. Norris described his pathway to

achieving multiple black belts, including those in Tang Soo Do, tae kwon do, and Shito-Ryu karate. Frankly, he inspired me to want to take my skills to the next level. I would have continued in karate except I was the only kid in the class who wore street clothes. I couldn't afford a Gi.

Mr. Freid said, "Sorry, no Gi, no Karate."

Chuck Norris's visit made me realize I wanted nothing to do with drugs, and that I could accomplish whatever I set my mind on doing. The fact that Mr. Norris didn't have a dad to show him the ropes didn't prevent him from climbing high and reaching the top in his field. As Mr. Norris bowed toward us, hands pressed together, I knew he was a man worthy of respect. The kind of guy I'd like to be. Definitely the warrior type King Arthur would break bread with.

After Chuck Norris left, Mr. Freid asked us to create a poster with some sort of antidrug headline. I decided to draw an overview shot of a Formula 1 racing car, which I was getting pretty good at. Across the top, I made up and inked the slogan, *Keep Speed on the Right Track*. I don't know how I knew what "speed" was. I just did. I probably heard about the drug from my older brothers and sisters.

I remember working on that poster at home until every inch was perfect. I was proud of the final product and knew in my heart that if Chuck Norris could see it, he'd agree it was ad agency quality. *Who knows,* I thought, *maybe he'd even want to use it in his antidrug talks.* When I turned in the poster, I didn't expect Mr. Freid to ask me to stay after class. When he did, I figured he was going to tell me how wonderful my poster was—or that he planned to show it to his famous karate buddy.

"Son, have a seat." It wasn't a suggestion. He parked his frame against the edge of the desk and I complied. His arms bulged when he folded them together.

"Jimmy, do you know what plagiarism is?"

I offered a blank stare. "No. Should I?"

He plucked my poster off the top of the desk and tilted it forward like a lawyer making his case before the judge. This was Exhibit A.

"Plagiarism is when you pass someone's idea off as your own. You *did* know that your slogan was supposed to be an original idea, right?"

I nodded, unsure what the problem was.

"So, where did you get yours from?"

I didn't know what to say. I mean, my teacher, a man whom I respected and admired, who just so happened to be a policeman, was telling me that I had stolen something—plagiarized the idea or whatever. But I didn't steal it.

"Mr. Freid, I made it up, honestly."

"You're in sixth grade, Jimmy," he said, letting the poster fall back against the desk. "How do you know anything about a hard drug like speed?"

When I told Mr. Freid that I didn't know how I knew about speed, that I must have heard about it from my older siblings, he didn't buy it. And, he maintained that I must have stolen the slogan for my poster. Mr. Freid doubted my honesty and his lack of faith crushed me. It wasn't my creativity that was in question; it was my integrity. When Marky Reil called me a liar, I could handle that because I didn't respect him. But when Mr. Freid didn't believe I was telling the truth, it completely undid me.

I'd like to tell you there was a happy, fairy-tale ending, that Mr. Freid later believed me and awarded me a prize for my outstanding poster—an autographed Gi from Chuck Norris or something. But that's not the way it happened. In fact, just when I thought things couldn't get any worse, they did.

# Journey's End

Nothing about the wallet was particularly remarkable. That is, nothing except for the circumstances under which it was found. The wallet was brown, a threefold case purchased more for function than style. According to the faded gold foil stamping along its edge, the billfold was made from "100% Genuine Imitation Leather."

The wallet rested, flaps open, on the kitchen table with its inner chambers methodically emptied of their contents. Adjacent to the billfold was a driver's license, social security card, a couple of credit cards, and a number of wallet-sized photos arranged faceup. If the items had been tossed haphazardly, it would have suggested a robbery. Instead, these personal effects were arranged systematically in two orderly rows.

The wallet was discovered just after lunch on a Friday. A single, tarnished brass key, evidently no longer necessary to perform its duty, rested to the left of the identification. While no note was left nearby explaining the enigma, the staging suggested that a statement had nevertheless been intended by the owner. Dee Dee was the first to stumble upon our dad's wallet. Now seventeen and soon to be eighteen, she was in the process of moving to her own apartment. Having inherited her work ethic from my mom, Dee Dee had graduated from high school a year early and taken a job at an insurance company. That Friday afternoon she'd returned to collect a few remaining possessions, but got more than she bargained for.

Trying to make sense out of what the array of Dad's things might mean, Dee Dee reached out and, with a careful eye, studied the items one by one. When no plausible explanation came to mind, she snatched the phone and dialed Kim.

"Hey, Sis," Kim said. "What's up?"

"I just stopped by the apartment and … well … do you know where Dad is?"

"On a Friday? He'd be at work, right?"

"That's what I thought …" Dee Dee's voice trailed off.

"You sound worried. What is it?"

"Just that … this is *so* bizarre." Dee Dee hooked her hair behind her left ear. "Maybe it's nothing, but I found his wallet and the apartment key on the kitchen table. What do you think that means?"

"Could he have forgotten to take them to work?"

"I don't think so, Kim." Dee Dee lifted the driver's license and studied the photo. "I mean, it's totally empty, and all of his ID was just laid out in rows on the table."

Kim absorbed that piece of the puzzle. "Maybe he was drying them out, you know, if he'd spilled a beer on them or something," Kim said, then paused as if weighing the likelihood of that scenario. She added, "Did you see him? Are you sure he's not there?"

"No. Hold on."

Dee Dee held the receiver to her chest and called his name. When Dad didn't answer, she put the phone down and did a hurried sweep of the place. She retrieved the phone.

"He's not here."

"What about Jimmy?"

"No, he's at school. Now what?"

"Call Dave, call Mike. See if they know what's up."

"Sure … I just don't have a good feeling about this, Kim."

"What do you mean?"

"Well … did Dad just leave us?"

A silence fell between them. Kim said, "If he did, he'd have taken his wallet, right?"

"My point exactly. So …"

"Is there anything missing?"

Dee Dee glanced around. "Doesn't look like it. Look, I'll call the guys and get back to you, okay?"

Dee Dee returned the phone to the cradle with a soft click. She stared at the table, momentarily paralyzed by what this turn of events might mean. When she was younger, long before I was born, Dad would disappear unannounced, sometimes for weeks at a time. The fact that he might be up to his old tricks concerned her, especially now that she'd moved out. She knew if Dad had hopped a train or a bus to Reno or Las Vegas to gamble, he'd be back.

One problem. I'd be alone in the apartment until he returned, perhaps days later. But that disappearing act reflected his past behavior, not Dad's somewhat more responsible actions of late. And Dad would have taken his wallet and key with him had he gone on a trip. Leaving those things behind made no sense … *unless* … she leaned on the chair back to steady herself. What if Dad had no intention of returning because he'd be *unable* to return?

Could that be it?

Had someone or something from his past caught up with him? Had he become so distressed that he concluded life wasn't worth living? Whatever my dad's reason for disappearing, Dee Dee had to immediately address the fact that I was uncared for.

She had reached for the phone to call Dave when the apartment door opened.

## DEAD MAN WALKING

At the sound of the door swinging on its hinges, Dee Dee jumped from the chair, almost tipping it over in the process. Dad stood at the threshold, apparently as startled to see Dee Dee as she was to see him. A blanket, hastily gathered together and tucked under his left arm, made him appear as if he had returned from a picnic. His pants were stained with dirt at the knees as if he'd slid into home plate. His shirt was disheveled, partially untucked at the belt. He seemed momentarily disoriented as if he had returned from an alternate reality.

He took several steps into the room before speaking.

"I see you found my things."

Dee Dee's face flushed. She felt an odd mixture of guilt and relief; she was relieved to see Dad, but felt a twinge of guilt over prying through his personal stuff. She found her legs and hurried to his right side for a hug. His stance stiffened the moment she wrapped her arms around him, as if he were hiding something.

"I was so worried, Dad."

"Really? About what?"

For a split second, Dee Dee wondered if she had misread the significance of discovering his wallet and key. Had she overreacted and let her imagination get the better of her? Might there be a perfectly harmless explanation? She decided to press him.

"Well, for one thing, Dad, why was all of your ID just laid out on the table like that? Doesn't that seem odd?"

"If it's all the same to you, I'd rather not talk about it." He dropped the blanket on the floor and headed to the kitchen. She followed him and leaned against the counter while he retrieved a beer from the refrigerator.

"Come on, Dad. You don't look so good. Where've you been?"

He twisted off the top and took a swig from the bottle. "The park."

"The park? With a blanket? What for? Aren't you supposed to be at work?" Her words came out sounding more accusing than she felt.

Blank stare. He was somewhere on the dark side of the moon and she didn't know how to reach him. She softened her voice and tried again.

"Look, Dad, I understand this might not be easy for you … but if you at least tell me what's going on … maybe there's a way I can help."

Another swallow of beer. He looked up from his bottle and searched her eyes as if questioning her capacity to hear what he had to say. Dee Dee was always very levelheaded and more mature for her age than her peers. He must have known that creating an elaborate fabrication wouldn't work with her. That, or he'd lost the will to fight.

"The truth?"

"That would be nice," she said with a nod.

Dad slouched into a chair at the kitchen table. Dee Dee pulled up a seat across from him. Picking at the edge of the label on his beer, he started to peel away the foil. He pursed his mouth and blew out a long, restless breath.

"I … look, there's no easy way to say this."

His eyes seemed to go out of focus. A moment later, he bit his bottom lip and started to study the contour of the beer bottle, as if peering into the amber glass would help him gather his thoughts. Dee Dee waited. She didn't understand the mind of an alcoholic, even after so many years of having two parents who struggled to remain sober. At the same time, she knew enough not to stifle him with too many interruptions.

"Look, I went to the park because … I didn't want to live anymore." His eyes met hers, then he quickly looked away, embarrassed by the confession. Dad shifted in his chair. His shoulders drooped forward. He was a defeated man. Dee Dee felt the air start to burn in her lungs.

"I took the blanket to cover up after … you know, after I cut my wrists. I didn't want to make a scene." He drained the bottle and then slumped against the chair back. "Obviously, I couldn't go through with it."

The room felt unusually warm. Dee Dee began to feel lightheaded, as if her world had just spun out of its orbit. Her throat, now dry as the desert, wouldn't allow her to form a response. She swallowed, hard. Even though he was just across the table, she had the urge to run to his side and comfort him. She wanted to hug him with an embrace that would forever wipe away the sadness he wore on his face. She heard herself say two words.

"Why, Dad?"

"I guess … well, living with you and Jimmy reminded me of what I had." He paused. "I lost everything after Mom took you guys away."

"You're blaming Mom?" Dee Dee said.

He waved her off. "No. Your mom did what she had to do. I know that." He closed his eyes for a moment. When he reopened them, tears formed at the edges. "I had it all and blew it. How does a man live with that?"

Dee Dee had some appreciation for the depth of his regret. Right before Mom died, Dee Dee and Kim risked the wrath of Hank the Tank by breaking into Mom's bedroom to talk. They laid down next to Mom and during those few intimate moments, Mom said, "Girls, all I ever wanted to do was to be a good mom, a good wife, make breakfast, help you with your schoolwork, take care of your clothes, and keep the house clean." That's exactly what Dad had wanted too, but the only time they had ever been happy was when we lived on Cosby Street.

But Dad's drinking had burned the last bridge home. He lost the only thing that was important to him—his family. As much as Dee Dee wanted Dad to be strong and to assure her everything would be okay, he didn't have the strength or the will left in him to fight. Dad needed to get help. Having his kids back home should have been a good thing, but Dee Dee was convinced Dad couldn't handle the pressure—or the memories of the better times.

"We'll get through this, Dad," she said, with a pat to the back of his hand. How they'd get through it, she wasn't sure. The last thing she wanted to do was to leave me alone with Dad, now that he was drinking more heavily and had come close to attempting suicide. Slipping out of his chair, Dad stood then returned to the refrigerator for another beer.

"I guess you're gonna tell the others, right?"

## READY, FIRE, AIM

My siblings were quick to lobby me with their laundry list of concerns. I understood their misgivings. Living with Dad wasn't wise, they said. What if I came home from school one day and found that my father had committed suicide in the apartment? I was only twelve. He was unstable, unpredictable, unreliable, and definitely making unhealthy choices. He didn't seem interested in getting help for his drinking. They were convinced that things *had* to change before something dreadful happened.

In spite of their concerns, I didn't want to leave my dad. I understood my siblings were looking after my best interests, but I loved Dad. And I'd already been through so much. The death of my mother. Hank leaving us. The Reils. The excitement of being reunited with Dad. And now they had this notion that I should check out of his world because he had issues. The thought of yet another change was too much for me to handle.

Adding insult to injury, they wanted *me* to break the bad news to Dad—and the sooner the better. That broke my heart. Why did I have to do the dirty work? I felt sure my dad would get the impression that I didn't love him because I was leaving him. Nothing could be further from the truth. I did love him. He wasn't perfect. Far from it. But he was *my* dad.

Yet, once again, what choice did I have?

The inevitable family meeting was called. I dreaded that day as if it were a date with the hangman. Dad, Mike, Dave, Dee Dee, Kim, and I sat in a circle at my brother Dave's house in Yucca Valley. When Dee Dee and I moved in with Dad, Dave had stayed behind at the Reils' to work. Dave, who was twenty at the time, got married to a minor and had a baby. They rented a modest house on Cherokee Street, which now hosted our family summit.

The drapes were drawn to protect us from the uncharitable afternoon desert sun. The air felt stuffy. The swamp cooler strained to provide some relief. Although the room was sparsely furnished with little more than a couch, a TV, and the extra chairs rounded up for the group, I felt as though the walls were closing inward. The thought of dismissing my father from my life was overwhelming.

More than anything, the finality of announcing the decision was weighing on me. Like a drowning man hanging onto a plank for dear life, I didn't want to let go of my dad. I had the sinking feeling Dad would hear the news and sail out of my life forever. But, since I was only twelve, I was following the leadership of my older siblings. I was also troubled because I wasn't sure anybody had the presence of mind to lay out a strategy or think through the issues of my long-term care beforehand. I was about to cut my ties to Dad without a backup plan.

After a little chitchat, we got down to the matter at hand. I'm sure Dad must have had an idea why the meeting had been called. At least he didn't appear startled when the conversation was directed to the topic of his drinking, his behavior, and its impact on me since I was living under the same roof. While I don't remember the exact flow of the conversation, I'll never forget when Mike, sitting across the room from me, said, "So, Jimmy, what's your decision?"

D-Day had arrived and I was about to drop the bomb. I turned, looked at my dad, and hesitated. I knew once I spoke the words I'd practiced in my head, there would be no going back. I didn't know a broken heart could beat so hard. Somehow I found the words. "Dad, I don't … I don't think it's a good idea to, well, to live with you anymore." The words seemed to hang in the air.

Dad scratched the side of his head and asked me something that I didn't anticipate. "Why?"

I was caught off guard. I'd practiced reciting my one-sentence statement, but I wasn't prepared for a follow-up question. I couldn't think of a good answer. I actually *did* want to live with him. I'd only said that I didn't because that's what was expected of me.

Finally, a bold thought hit my mind. I blurted out: "Because of all the stuff you did to Mom." There was definitely real hard truth behind those words. To his credit, Dad didn't attempt to shift the blame or dodge what had happened in the past. With a nod, he said,

"I can accept that. I wasn't a good husband or father."

The meeting ended abruptly and Dad stood to leave. I was so emotionally wrung out that I actually forgot to hug him good-bye. Noticing the oversight, Mike came to me and said, "You should hug Dad. It might be the last time you hug him." Still numb from the whole surreal experience, I complied. I crossed the room and gave him a hug more out of duty than passion. I felt neutral. Certainly not the way I felt during our embrace when I took a bus to see him, or the time I hugged him with uninhibited joy when he arrived at the Reils'.

Even with all of my practice, I never got used to saying good-bye.

Although I managed to survive that confrontation, there was no concrete decision as to where I'd live. Afterward, since I wasn't returning to San Gabriel with my dad, Dave pulled me aside and told me I had two options. I could throw myself on the mercy of the foster-care system—although, speaking from his personal experience back when Dad and Mom were too drunk to care for him, he didn't think that was such a great idea. "Or," Dave said, with a squeeze to my shoulder, "why don't you move in with me?"

Dave was gracious to make the offer and I accepted his hospitality. He was always good about trying to keep us together. Although a disaster, the experience at the Reils' was Dave's way of keeping us a family. Now, once again, he was taking the lead and holding things together. I never did return to my dad's place.

Dave retrieved my stuff from my dad's, and I started my life sharing the cramped quarters with Dave and his wife, who interestingly was named Dee, and their infant, Kelly. What made this arrangement somewhat ... *unusual* ... was the age difference between myself, at twelve years old, and Dee, who was sixteen. My new foster mom was just four years older than me. Considering how unorthodox my life had been to date, I guess just about nothing fazed me.

## THE END GAME

While I was getting settled at Dave's place, my father, rather than live alone, agreed to move in with Mike. Having finished his service in the navy, Mike was attending the University of Nevada in Reno, and playing on the football team. For his part, Dad used his social security checks to drink and play the slots. On hindsight, considering that Dad was a gambler and Reno was a gambling town, that wasn't the best idea in the long run. But it was his choice.

One evening, Mike came home to his apartment and found Dad seriously drunk. Dad could get mean when under the influence of alcohol, as we learned in the hammer house. It didn't help matters that Mike and Dad had their share of confrontations over the years. Had we considered the wisdom of pairing the two of them together, a different arrangement might have been advisable. While they didn't come to fists, the heated skirmish placed Dad on a course of action from which there'd be no return.

This particular night, Mike confronted my dad about his unacceptable behavior. Between making his grades at school, working two jobs, and tackling the grueling football schedule, Mike was under a great deal of pressure. Pulling the extra weight of a drunk was more than he could handle. Mike said, "Dad, I can't keep this up. I can't keep living this way with you drunk all of the time. I refuse to support your habit."

That was like throwing fuel on the fire. Enraged at the thought that he was some kind of a burden to Mike, Dad took a $100 bill from his wallet and threw it at Mike, saying, "Here then, take this blankety-blank money" (only he had filled in the blanks). Exercising an amazing amount of restraint, Mike said, "Look, Dad, I don't want your money. I just want you to be sober. If you can't sober up, I'll find you another place." Rather than return to Alcoholics

Anonymous, Dad said, "Then, I guess I don't need to be here."

Mike found a nearby one-room studio and paid for three months rent up front. Dad stayed all of three weeks and didn't return. Every time Mike would stop by to check on him, the landlady said she hadn't seen our dad in a long while. She finally decided to box up Dad's few possessions and re-rent the room. When Mike checked in one last time, he learned that Dad did finally stop by. He collected his things and the unused portion of the rent money, and then disappeared. We had no idea where he went.

Several months later, I was lying on the couch at Dave's house watching the *I Love Lucy* show. I wasn't a big fan, it just happened to be on after dinner. I was doing well in my studies and in sports. Living with Dave and Dee seemed to be working out. Sure, we had our struggles, but unlike with the Reils, the feeling in the home was calm. Dee was very kind toward me and took the new living situation in stride. It was November and we hadn't heard from Dad in months, but that wasn't a surprise.

The phone rang.

Dave, who was closest to the kitchen, picked up after several rings and listened. Although I continued to watch TV, I sensed that something about Dave's demeanor had changed—almost as if an invisible fog settled over him. Since the phone cord was long enough to stretch to the dining room table, Dave took a seat as he continued to listen. He said little and, within a few minutes, hung up.

"Jimmy," he called.

"Yeah?"

"Dad's dead."

Still lounging on the couch, I looked over my shoulder and said, "Oh, that's too bad." I really didn't feel anything. No waves of sadness. No tears. I was numb. I realize that may sound coldhearted. Maybe I had prepared myself for the worst for quite some time.

Dave clicked off the TV and said, "Jimmy … you okay?"

"Sure." In truth, it would take three full years for my tears to force their way out of the vault where I had safely tucked away my feelings.

"That was Mike."

"Really? Was he with Dad?"

"No. Mike said he was playing football when his coach asked him if he knew where Dad was." Dave pulled up a seat. "Mike said that was strange since he never talked about Dad with the coach before." Dave, clearly more shaken by the news than I was, went on to recite the conversation between Mike and his coach.

Mike had said, "He's dead, isn't he?"

The coach was startled by Mike's quick assessment. "Why do you say that?"

Mike said, "Because he was a drunk and a bum."

The coach told Mike they'd received a call from the coroner and that Mike needed to go downtown to identify the body. Mike went to the police station and said, "I'm Mike Daly. My dad was found someplace. I'd like to know where."

He was told, "You really don't want to know."

Mike replied, "I'll make that decision."

They explained that a twelve-year-old boy discovered Dad's body in an abandoned Laundromat warehouse building across the street from the police station. Dad evidently died of hypothermia. Unlike Mom, who had her children and her loved ones around her as death approached, Dad died alone.

After identifying our dad's body, Mike went to see where Dad had been living. The building had no electricity, no heat, and was strewn with litter. Dad had made the corner of an office his "home" with little more than a dirty, beat-up old mattress and a few personal effects in a paper bag.

His wallet was never found.

I would later learn that Dad had been placed in a paupers casket, which was essentially a cardboard box. Dave, Mike, and a woman official from the funeral home, whose name I never learned, conducted the service. My sister Dee Dee was almost eight months pregnant and wasn't permitted to make the trip. Kim was at a Palm Springs hospital with her husband who had a hernia operation and couldn't break free.

I don't think anybody thought about me going.

In the end, my father was buried by two sons who really didn't like him that much and a stranger. There had been no talk of faith, no minister offering assurances of him being in a better place, and certainly not the crowd of well-wishers who wanted to honor his life as hundreds had done for my mother. The contrast couldn't have been greater.

I couldn't help but wonder why his life had to end that way. He knew that my mom gave her heart to God just before passing into eternity. What prevented him from doing the same? Pride? Ego? Fear? One thing was certain: Having watched the way my mom and my dad had lived and died, I knew which example I wanted to follow.

There was, however, one bright spot. After the burial service, such as it was, Mike and Dave learned that Dad had been volunteering at the Good Shepherd Lutheran Church not far from the warehouse where he'd been found. The church folks loved him and appreciated the way he'd show up day after day to help out with their programs.

Was it possible that Dad had a change of heart?

# 12

# Holy Huddle

Not long after my father died, I turned thirteen and my body became a stranger to me. With puberty, the rules of the universe seemed to change overnight. I started to sprout hair where none had been before. I was introduced to a razor, underarm deodorant, and mouthwash. I became self-conscious around the girls at school who, up until then, suffered from that contagious disease called "cooties." For reasons I couldn't explain, I found myself suddenly fascinated by God's fairest creation and actually enjoying their company.

Unfortunately, at the most inconvenient times, like talking to those newly discovered cute girls or answering a question in class, my voice developed a mind of its own. I'd start to speak when, without notice, my vocal cords would betray me with honking sounds like those played by first-year clarinet students. I could hide my sweaty palms and racing heartbeat, but that caterwauling always brought snickers.

I was regularly making the honor roll at school, but my transformation from boyhood to manhood required some coaching. Now that Dad was dead, I suppose I was looking for someone—a man—to be a role model, or at least a friend. About that time, my brother Dave's wife, Dee, was paid a visit by her older brother, Ronnie

Hughes. I immediately thought I found someone with whom I could connect.

In some respects, Ronnie reminded me of my dad. Both men were athletic. Both loved baseball. Ronnie had played baseball for the University of California at Irvine the year they won the NCAA (National Collegiate Athletic Association) championship. He was such a good athlete that he went on to play for an Angels farm team. So, when Ronnie invited me to play catch just before sundown one evening, I was thrilled.

Of course, at the time I agreed, I'd never witnessed the fury of a ninety-five-mile-per-hour fastball. Ronnie was a pitcher with a rocket launcher for an arm. Not only did the ball sail into my mitt as fast as a shooting star, he threw what he called a "rising fastball." This ball moved like nothing I'd ever seen. It took all of the focus I had to keep up with him.

When his mom called out that dinner was about ready, we agreed he'd throw one more pitch. Ronnie fired a missile that tailed up suddenly, clipping the edge of my glove. Bouncing off my mitt, the leather fireball hit me square in the cheekbone, totally shattering the left side of my face.

I thought I was dying. Like slamming a car door on your fingers, waves of pain surged from my head through my body, practically sending me into shock. Trying to cope with this sensory overload, my enflamed network of nerves started shutting down as if a thick curtain of numbness had been pulled across my face. I was in a fog. Blood began to pour out of my mouth and nose.

I was rushed to the hospital where I spent two weeks undergoing, and healing from, extensive reconstructive surgery. I later learned that I had a broken nose, broken cheek, broken eye socket, busted jaw, and fractured skull. Ronnie's pitch was so hard, you could see the imprint of the baseball stitches welded into my cheek for days. On the upside, I was excused from school for several weeks—that part was a nice change of pace.

Interestingly, I can't remember blaming God for this accident or for any of the hard breaks along my journey. My prevailing attitude was that "things just happen."

My doctor informed me that, had the baseball made contact an inch and a half to the right, it would have killed me. Thirteen-year-olds typically think they're invincible and don't spend a lot of time dwelling on death or dying, but his assessment was a wake-up call. One minute I was playing baseball, the next minute I could have been dead. I had to wonder, was God trying to tell me something?

Although I was young, I had an acute sense that this life wasn't the end of the story. Death was all too real to me, having lost both parents. Now my own close encounter prompted me to do some heavy-duty thinking. I felt pretty sure another chapter would be written once I stepped across the threshold of life and into eternity. Grandpa Hope seemed convinced that giving your heart to God was important—a step I hadn't made and didn't know how to make. Lying there wrapped in bandages like a mummy, I had more questions than answers.

Thoughts of death and the afterlife aside, I was so banged up that two officers from the San Bernardino sheriff's office came to my hospital room to investigate the cause of my injuries. They said, "Jim, we don't think you've been straight with us. Given the extent of your injuries, we think you've been involved in a gang fight. We believe this was no accident. Were you, in fact, hit by a baseball bat? Are you lying to us to cover it up? Nobody gets this hurt just playing catch. What gang did this?" When I explained that Ronnie was a pitcher who played college baseball and spent time in the Angels organization, it seemed to placate them. They closed their notebooks and left.

The force of the ball actually cut the ganglion, a group of nerve cells, leaving the left side of my face numb. To this day, my teeth, my cheek, and my lips on the left side have no feeling aside from a minor tingle. As skilled as my doctor was, he wasn't certain whether my damaged nerves would heal properly. Back then, there were no precision microsurgery techniques that increase the odds of a successful outcome. Thankfully, I did get some movement back in my upper lip after the surgery.

It's worth jumping ahead of the story for a moment. Several years later, I had turned sixteen and was sitting in algebra class daydreaming about dating Cheryl Wheeler. Cheryl and I had known each other since the second grade when we attended Yucca Valley Elementary School together. Although I had changed schools several times, when I moved back to Yucca Valley to live with Dave, we were reacquainted. Now I couldn't take my eyes off of her. Cheryl was terminally cute. She had flowing brunette hair that smelled of roses when she walked by and a smile so warm it could melt snow. She and about three other girls were *the* "catch" of the class.

I was really out of my league, reaching for the top.

I'd always wanted to ask Cheryl out for a date. We were friends, but I hoped there could be more between us. The fact that we were assigned seats side by side in the front row of class had to be a signal that we were destined to be together, right? I remember thinking, *This is it. I'm going to ask Cheryl out Friday night for a date.* Since my desk was on the far left row adjacent to the wall, my left side, the numb side, wasn't actually seen by anybody unless I turned my head.

I mustered all of the courage I could summon, took a quick breath to settle my nerves, then turned to look at the angelic being sitting three feet from me. I said, "Hey, Cheryl, do you want to go out Friday night?" She took one look at me … and started chuckling—not a mean, black-hearted laugh. It was more of a musical chuckle. I flushed and felt like Bozo the Clown.

I thought, *What's going on? Did I say something funny?* I can't say that I could see anything humorous about my question. Seeing my dream girl grin and point toward my face made me think of an explanation. I turned away and touched my upper lip on the left side of my mouth.... My hunch was confirmed: I had something moist streaming down my lip from my nose, only I hadn't felt it because my face was numb. If the floor would have opened up at that moment and swallowed me, I would have been eternally grateful. I was so embarrassed. I slumped back into my seat.

She allowed me a minute to collect myself. I walked up to the teacher's desk where Mrs. Pruett kept a box of Kleenex for students in need. When I returned to my seat, Cheryl simply turned toward me with that great smile and said, "I'm sorry, Jim. I'm busy Friday night." In my view, that was close enough to the familiar brush-off, "I gotta wash my hair tonight."

Now my face *and* my heart were broken.

Not long after recovering from my accident, my brother Dave and his wife, Dee, started to have marital difficulties. Considering how young they were, I wasn't surprised. I don't know all the reasons, but they simply did not have enough life experience under their belts to sustain them when things got tough. After four years together, they divorced. Dee moved out, and Dave and I became bachelor roommates. I washed my own clothes, paid bills, worked a job at the Dairy Queen cleaning fry vats and windows, went to school ... and wondered if there were good guys in the world who modeled what being a man was all about.

177

## FOOTBALL FAITH

Most of the men in my life didn't have their acts together: drugs, alcohol, addictions, poor judgment—I'd seen it all. True, Mr. Freid, my sixth-grade homeroom teacher back at my old school—the one with the black belt and Chuck Norris as a friend—was a rare exception. But even Mr. Freid had basically accused me of lying and refused to take me at my word. I still held that as a disappointment.

God must have known the longing of my heart because a surprise was waiting for me in 1976 when I returned for my second year of high school football. Everyone was talking about the new coach, Paul Moro. A graduate of Long Beach State, Paul played linebacker and was selected to the collegiate All-American First Team along with notables like star quarterback Pat Haden. Pat led his University of Southern California team to three Rose Bowl contests and went on to play for the NFL's Los Angeles Rams.

Paul was a little undersized to pursue a professional football career and, instead, wanted to invest his life coaching high school football—and mentoring young men. We were the first team he coached. Strolling onto the field, I got the impression "Coach Mo" was a real tough, no-nonsense kind of guy. Fit, blond, and tan, with sunglasses and white sunscreen on his lips to block the sun, he commanded our attention—and got it.

Coach Mo and I immediately clicked. He became my first true mentor and got involved in the details of my life. As we got to know each other that first semester, Coach Mo and his wife, Joyce, reached out to me, inviting me to their house for dinner from time to time. They were so … *normal*. I'd forgotten what normal was, considering that the last time I'd experienced an intact family situation was when I was four. It felt good. Very good. Almost scary good. Brokenness I understood. "Normal" was just not in my vocabulary.

On the field, Coach Mo pushed me toward excellence. He'd say, "Jim, you need to be the leader. I want you to set the example. Be the first to finish the wind sprints and show the others how to hustle." I liked that. I appreciated the fact that Coach saw me as a natural leader. Talk about a real confidence builder. He knew how to bring the best out of me.

Not only was he a rock-solid man, I learned that Coach Mo was a man with deep moral convictions. Faith in God was a big part of his life. I'd never really met anyone like him before and wanted to understand how a burly linebacker could believe in something—in Someone—whom he couldn't see. When I said as much, Coach invited me to go with him and several others from our team to a football camp sponsored by the Fellowship of Christian Athletes.

I was curious to find out what faith and football had to do with each other. About fifty guys from several area schools loaded up in a parade of vans and headed to Point Loma College, an oceanfront college in San Diego. The days were structured around sharpening our football skills. For eight intense hours we worked on technique, conducted drills, scrimmaged, and listened to coaching instructors who gave us group and personal training.

At night, although exhausted and nursing our sore muscles, we were told to gather in a room to participate in something our leaders called "devotions." Most of us felt like collapsing in bed. I know I did. But we filed in anyway, grunting and groaning like trolls tromping home from a brutal day at the coal mines. We flopped down on the floor like beached whales as the meeting was called to order.

Somebody with a guitar and an overhead projector did his best to get fifty ruff-n-tumble guys to sing along. At first, few took the bait. We were a tough crowd, beefy linebackers and all. I mean, the level of testosterone in that room must have exceeded the recommended limits allowable by law. More than anything, we macho teens didn't want to appear too eager to sing along. Singing was something girls did. Rather than risk public ridicule from our peers, most half-sung, half-mumbled through the tunes.

But the room seemed to fade around me when the guest speaker, whose name I don't recall, started his talk. I hung onto every word as he described the emptiness he felt in his life: how in spite of his accomplishments, and regardless of what he had tried, nothing seemed adequate to fill the void in his soul. I felt as if he were speaking to me because I knew that feeling all too well.

I figured a large part of that emptiness had to do with my transient home life. I had no stability. My life had been nothing more than a fragmented series of events, or so it seemed. And yet, as this speaker talked about God's pursuit and His unconditional love, he began to untangle a mystery for me. I started to connect some of the dots and see glimpses of God's love at work throughout my life. For instance, it was no accident that God had brought people of faith like Coach Mo into my life.

Sitting on the floor, listening and yet reflecting, I remembered Grandpa Hope had described Mom feeling that there was something missing in her life too. And how, when given the chance, she invited God into her heart. She was with God, according to Grandpa. That memory reminded me of the clouds forming a stairway to heaven in the sky at Mom's graveside service, and, for the first time, I made a connection. Was God saying Mom had taken a step of faith that I, too, would one day take? Maybe.

I also thought about how I felt God's presence when I cried out to Him sitting on the sand hill in fourth grade and how God had spared me from being shot by Wild Bill or being killed by a fastball. Considering my path in light of what the speaker was saying, I got the distinct impression that God was pursuing me. He had never given up on me. All of those years I had been on a spiritual quest, but I hadn't recognized it for what it was.

The speaker finished his comments by reading a verse that says, "The thief comes only to steal and kill and destroy; I have come that they may have life, and have it to the full." That sounded good. Life to the full. No more emptiness. No more restlessness. No more wondering what would happen to me if I were to die. I knew right then that I wanted God to be a part of my life.

When he asked if anyone wanted to come to the front of the room to invite Jesus Christ into their life and have Him forgive their sin, I went forward. I could feel the eyes of the guys on me, but I didn't care. More than anything, I wanted peace within. Of course, the only prayer I knew was the one Hank the Tank taught us to pray at mealtimes: "Bless us, O Lord, for these thy gifts that we are about to receive from the hand of Christ our Lord, Amen." I was pretty sure this was different. Thankfully, one of the leaders put his arm around my shoulder and coached me through the biggest decision of my life.

In the days following my profession of faith, I sensed a change in my heart but I never experienced an epiphany. I didn't hear angelic music playing in my head, but still, I was different. Coach Mo noticed the change and was excited for me. Even though I had no clue what to do next, transformation was under way.

And that was good enough for me.


## DON'T LET IT HURT


Here's a perfect example of how I had begun to change on a spiritual level. By the time my senior year rolled around, I was heavily invested in football, which had become really important to me. I worked hard to be the starting quarterback. I spent long hours on the practice field perfecting my performance, and I pushed myself to be at the top of my game.

Thanks to efforts from my coach, I received letters of intent from the University of Nevada, Las Vegas; Texas Christian University; and a couple of other big-time college campuses. As far as I was concerned, the sky was royal blue. Nothing but clear sailing for me. Maybe I'd take a scholarship to one of the colleges courting me and then go on to play pro ball. Why not?

About that time, my brother Mike, who'd played defensive tackle for the University of Nevada at Reno, came to watch me play. Frankly, he didn't like what he saw. I mean, I played strong. He was impressed, but he was concerned about my arrogant behavior. After the game, Mike said, "Jim, you know what? You're getting a big head about playing football. You're not the same guy you used to be." His words hit me like a bucket of ice water in the face. I felt blitzed.

Normally, I would have ignored a comment like that. I might have dismissed it as jealousy or whatever. Instead, I reflected on Mike's concern in light of my commitment to the Lord. Rather than disregard Mike's insight, I decided to pray. I said, "Lord, what does this mean? Has football become an obsession? Should I give it up?" I wrestled with Mike's assessment because I didn't want to have this ego thing going on. At the same time, I really loved the game and belonging to the team.

That's when I heard God speak. Not an audible voice, mind you. Rather, I had a sense, or maybe an impression, that continuing in the direction I was heading wouldn't be healthy. I began to entertain the unthinkable—maybe I should give up the game? And yet, since I was such a young believer, I wasn't sure God would ask me to do something so radical.

Did He really want me to give up football?

Two events cemented His answer for me. The first sign came when I separated my right shoulder on a fluke play. I had been hit by a defensive lineman when we were out of bounds—a hit that should never have happened. That injury took me out of play for a month, giving me plenty of time to gain some much-needed perspective. I came off the injured list just in time for our first league game. The feeling around town seemed to be, "Daly's back and we're gonna win."

Before the game I knelt down and prayed. I said, "Lord, if you don't want me to play big-time college football, break a bone today … but please don't let it hurt." You see, one of my early lessons as a young believer was that you've got to be careful what you pray—careful *and* specific. Big, general prayer requests leave too much room for interpretation. Instinctively, I must have known that I needed to be specific when I prayed about the matter of pain.

Rather than praying that God would break a bone but not let it hurt, I could have asked for something that didn't involve breaking a body part, like having it rain at halftime. I'm not typically a glutton for punishment. But so much was on the line—my entire career in football—that I guess I wanted there to be no wiggle room to explain away whether or not God did, in fact, answer my prayer.

In the third quarter of the game, one of our running backs was ejected for throwing a punch—the only time in my four years of playing high school football that a member of our team had been thrown out during a game. That was odd. The coach decided to bring in Parrish Robbins, a sophomore, to play fullback. We quickly huddled and I called the play—a straight, drop-back pass. I could tell by Parrish's eyes, wide as saucers, that he didn't know what to do. I told him to step to my right and hit anybody inside out.

The roar in the stadium reached a fevered pitch as we lined up for the second-down play. I took the snap, dropped back, and saw my receiver going deep. I waited for him to hit his mark downfield. Out of the corner of my eye, I noticed that the outside linebacker was charging toward me like a bull. Whether it was fear or a bad case of the jitters, Parrish didn't even touch him. He let out a "Whoah!" and then actually jumped out of the linebacker's way.

The guy creamed me.

I went down as he hit me underneath the shoulder, driving through the armpit. My first thought was that my separated shoulder injury was toast. As I pulled myself up from the turf, my right shoulder appeared to be fine, but something was wrong with my left arm. While it didn't hurt, I did feel a dull pressure. I reached under my shoulder pad and felt that my collarbone was broken. I could actually feel the points of the bone pushing up under the skin.

We huddled up again and I said, "Guys, I think God is answering my prayer."

That got a look from the team. They said, "What do you mean? Are we going to score a touchdown?"

I said, "No, I broke my collarbone."

More puzzled looks. Someone finally asked the obvious, "What kind of prayer is that?"

"I'll tell you later," I said, glancing toward the sideline. Evidently, the coach didn't notice how severely I'd been hit. Rather than make a scene, I sprinted off the field and told the team trainer that I thought I broke my collarbone. He sat me out for the third-down play. When we didn't get enough yardage for the first down, the head coach yelled over to me, "Daly! You gotta get in there and kick the ball," since I was also the team punter.

As I went to put on my helmet, I found that I couldn't raise my left arm hardly at all. It had been a few minutes so my left arm was kind of getting locked. Taking my position for the kick, I thought,

*Boy, this better be a good snap.* Fortunately, the snapper hit me right in the chest. I was able to catch the ball with one hand and make the kick. Even before the play downfield was finished, I walked off the field unable to continue.

I had my answer. I had broken a bone and it didn't hurt. That day was the last time I put on a uniform. Through that experience, I felt God as a father. It was as though He had whispered, "You know what, Jim, I appreciate that you stopped to ask Me which direction to go. I've answered your prayer." Isn't that amazing? That experience was a dramatic start to a lifelong pursuit of discovering God's agenda and putting it ahead of my own. Thankfully, it's the only time that broken bones were part of the discovery process—at least so far.

# Finally Home

I t would be difficult to top the craziness that characterized the first fifteen years of my home life. By the time I started my senior year in high school, I'd experienced just about every imaginable variation of home life as a child. I lived in a two-parent household, which, five years later, became a single-parent home led by Mom. With Hank the Tank, I experienced a stepfather running the home. I had a taste of foster care at the Reils'. I lived with my dad as the single parent, then shared a roof with my brother Dave and his wife. I also lived briefly with my unmarried sister, Dee Dee. Interestingly, I once counted and discovered that I'd lived in almost two dozen different houses or apartments along the way.

While moving around might not sound that unusual today, back then society was much more stable. Families stayed put. For better or worse, you had the same neighbors for years, even decades. On the positive side, families developed a network of friendships. You had a sense of belonging, of roots, of security.

While I had no idea what that feeling of continuity felt like, something inside of me longed for a place to call home. However, when I turned seventeen, I was out on my own. No parents. No contact with my siblings. Just me. My brother Dave and I had lived together as bachelors, but parted ways not long after he remarried. Let's just say that his new wife didn't warm to the idea of having "the kid brother around." I think she resented the fact that Dave insisted on taking me under his wing. When the tension reached a boiling point, I knew I needed to move on.

Thankfully, Joe and Ramona Campbell, the grandparents of my high school girlfriend, offered me a humble trailer, which was parked forty feet behind their home, under an oak tree. I was thrilled to have my "own" place to live.

The trailer was no more than 6' x 12' and was built by Joe years before. It was made out of wood with masonite exterior siding and an asphalt shingle roof. The inside featured dark pine paneling and shag orange carpet with a musty smell. I had one small window with a little drape over it. I had a space heater for cold nights, a bed, a small dresser, and that was about it. No phone. No refrigerator. No shower or running water. I went to the main house for those amenities.

But it was home.

Being around the Campbells was surprisingly comforting. I remember coming home late from football practice and sitting on the sofa with Ramona eating raisin toast. Together we'd snack and watch *The Tonight Show* starring Johnny Carson. You might say God was providing me with another glimpse of what "normal" family life felt like. When the program was over, she'd ask me about my day. We'd talk for a while, then I'd say "good night," brush my teeth, and go out to my trailer under the tree. Lying there in the dark, I'd think, *So, that's what a family is like.*

By the time I graduated from high school, I'd lived in twenty-three houses ... and one trailer. When I got the news that I'd earned a small scholarship for college, I thought things might start to turn around for me. And yet, I still kept my expectations low so I wouldn't be disappointed. The future felt like it could be promising. It had to be.

## COLLEGE BOUND

In the fall of 1979, I moved into a dorm on the campus of Cal State San Bernardino to start a new chapter in life. I was accepted to other universities, but I chose this school because it was close to the Campbells'. Their expression of kindness to me the previous year was one of the most gracious acts I'd ever experienced.

Although I hoped that this change would bring good things, I got off to a rough start. The freshman year of college is tough for students under normal circumstances. I didn't have parents to talk with about my class selection. I didn't have a home to go to for the weekend. Without the security that a family and a home provide, I couldn't shake the feelings of loneliness even though I was surrounded by thousands of students.

Making matters worse, I rather innocently alienated my professor of philosophy that first semester who, in turn, made my life in class miserable. It all started when my incoming freshman counselor said that, with my grade-point average, I should consider taking an upper-level class, a 300-level philosophy course even though I was just a freshman. With a class size of twenty, the setting was intimate and encouraged student-teacher interaction. I was told I'd have a great time.

From the first day, it was clear that my professor was enamored with the Greek philosophers Aristotle, Plato, and Socrates. He waxed eloquently about the wisdom of their teachings, the brilliance of the Socratic method, and recommended their writings as the key for achieving self-knowledge. I honestly wasn't attempting to start a brawl when I slipped up my hand and asked, "What about the words of Jesus?"

With that simple question, the professor became unhinged. I mean, he totally unraveled right before our eyes. Red in the face, he barked, "There's no evidence that Jesus ever lived. Most *intelligent* people know the Bible is nothing more than a myth … a compilation of stories that human beings want to believe about a perfect man to make themselves feel better."

For the next several minutes he railed against Jesus and the Bible with vein-popping anger. When I pushed back and asked a follow-up question, he unleashed his wrath on me. I ended up having to drop the course after about five classes because he appeared to enjoy ripping into me. Interestingly, that heated exchange put me on a journey of spiritual discovery that semester. I started reading about Aristotle and Plato, since they were held in such high esteem.

Probably my biggest surprise was learning that the earliest surviving copy of the writings of Aristotle was dated around 1,400 years after he lived. For Plato, the earliest surviving copy of his material was dated around 1,200 years after he lived. My professor had no problem referencing what these philosophers taught as fact—even though the only copies of their works were dated more than a thousand years after the original documents.

By contrast, regarding my professor's assertion that there was no evidence that Jesus existed, I found that there are over 24,000 manuscripts of various parts of the New Testament written by eyewitnesses who lived during the time of Jesus. Many wrote down their personal accounts within seventy years of His death. And, the oldest document of the New Testament we have today is a fragment of the gospel of

John written just twenty-nine years from the original.

I felt as if I'd caught my philosophy teacher being intellectually dishonest. He was unwilling to admit that Jesus lived, despite all of the eyewitness accounts. In my view, Jesus passed the test of historicity, and that knowledge grabbed me intellectually. While I had given my heart to God at age fifteen at the Fellowship of Christian Athletes football camp, I now realized that Jesus actually was who He said He was, and that His claims were backed up by the rules for measuring writings of antiquity.

That insight cemented my earlier step of faith and opened my heart to a deeper relationship with God. And, at the same time, I had a new thought. With all of the books I had been reading on the ancient philosophers, why wasn't I reading the most important book of all, namely, the Bible? Convicted, I sometimes played hooky from my classes to read the Bible for hours at a time.

While my spiritual life was slowly maturing, my sophomore year was the pits. I felt lost. I remember going to the counseling center to talk with a counselor. In addition to the questions common to freshmen, such as, "What am I doing?" "Who am I?" "Where am I going?" "What's life all about?" I needed to deal with my mom's death, my dad's death, and my crazy, mixed-up family life. More than anything, I needed a good cry. A hug.

And a place to call home.

Being homeless in college was no small deal. After I broke up with my girlfriend, I didn't feel comfortable visiting the Campbells' and staying in the trailer. I didn't think that would be fair to my ex-girlfriend and her family. So, during my sophomore year while living on campus, I had to apply for special permission to stay through the Christmas holiday in my dorm room. I was politely informed that the college shut down the dormitories and I would need to leave. When I explained that I didn't have anywhere to go, they made an exception. I was permitted to stay—with the understanding that there'd be no heat.

While friends were enjoying Christmas dinner and exchanging gifts with family and loved ones, I sat on the edge of my bed snacking on food from the vending machines. The campus was a ghost town. Walking the deserted streets at night was eerie and only reinforced my feelings of incredible isolation and loneliness—especially against the backdrop of the Christmas season. About all I could do was pour out my heart to God.

Here I was, the kid from Compton ... the little guy at the Reils' ... trailer boy. I thought that my life was quickly shaping up to be meaningless. Part of me desperately longed to travel—maybe study abroad and experience other cultures, but I figured that would never happen. I wasn't a fatalist. On the contrary, I was, and am, a very optimistic person. But that Christmas, I hit rock bottom. I felt trapped, stuck in a rut with no help of getting out. Even after reading in the school catalog about a study program in Japan for seniors, I shook my head in unbelief.

How could I ever afford to do that?

I won't suggest that I heard an audible voice, but something stirred in my heart. It felt as though God were saying, "Jim, trust Me." Of course, the fact that I had no money appeared to be an insurmountable obstacle. Then again, I had a lot to learn about God's endless resources and His ability to provide a way when, humanly speaking, I couldn't see a solution.

During my junior year, I visited with Ramona, whom I hadn't seen for a while. Just like the old times, we sat on the sofa, ate raisin toast, and watched Johnny Carson. Between the commercial breaks, I mentioned the idea of studying in Japan as a senior. Without hesitation, she offered to loan me the $5,000 necessary. I was floored. I really did not ask for or expect her help. But she and Joe were kind toward me. God, working through these dear friends, had answered my prayer. I only wished I could have called my mother with the great news.

## JAPAN WAS AH-SO GOOD

In 1982, I traveled to Tokyo to attend Waseda University, the Harvard of Japan. I was enrolled in their School of International Liberal Studies, also known as the Kokusaibu division and was assigned to live with a Japanese family who spoke very little English. The city of Tokyo is overwhelming in every way, even to the most seasoned traveler. With more than twelve million people, the city never sleeps. While I have many memories from that incredible experience, two are worth highlighting.

About three weeks into school, I remember sitting in my elementary Japanese language class. Our professor, Mr. Kobaiyashi, was a third-generation teacher who, like his grandfather and father before him, was writing his own English/Japanese dictionary. You might say he was a stickler for the correct usage of words. This particular day, he decided to use a new drill on us. Professor Kobaiyashi asked the class to construct a simple sentence in Japanese and express it aloud.

With three weeks of language training under our belts, none of us were very sharp. My classmates formed elementary sentences like, "See the dog run," or, "See the cat run," or, "See Spot run." Standing in the front of the class, Mr. Kobaiyashi would listen, correct their pronunciation or inflection, and then move on to the next student.

This particular day I had a severe headache. I thought it would be original if I translated the English sentence "Today, Teacher, I

193

have a terrible headache" into Japanese. When my turn came, I proudly said, *"Kiyo wa sensei, otama gai itai desu!"* Mr. Kobaiyashi immediately started laughing. Turning his face from the class, he composed himself, and then turned back to begin drilling the other students. *What did I say that was so funny?* I thought.

I wanted to ask him after class, but in the Japanese educational system you just don't have a relationship with the teacher as you might in the United States. The teacher-student relationship is much more formal. The minute I got home that night, I told my Japanese home mother what I had said in class. She started cracking up too—her eyes were even tearing up. Again, I was at a loss. What was so humorous about having a headache? Noticing my puzzled look, she got the cat and flipped it over. She pointed between its legs and smiled. Evidently, in perfect Japanese, I had said, "Today, Teacher, my testicles hurt."

Understanding the nuances of the language, while important, wasn't the main lesson I learned while studying in Japan. Experiencing another culture and seeing things that were so different from my limited vantage point as an American, especially in the area of faith, was fascinating. Shintoism teaches that you have to pay money for a good name so when you die you get closer to the Creator. It saddened me that poor people would pool their money to buy a name for their deceased loved ones. It also seemed suspicious that you had to pay the priest to get the name.

Learning about Shintoism, Buddhism, and Hinduism, all of which are a big part of the Asian cultures, actually helped me to go deeper in my understanding of why I believe what I believe. Rather than feel tempted to explore one of these Eastern religions, I found myself hungry to study the Bible. I would start reading the Bible and look up at the clock only to realize hours had passed.

I set myself up on a reading schedule and literally read, read, read the Bible every available moment I could. I was like a human sponge absorbing all of the insight I could get. I took breaks to attend class or go to a meal, and then returned to my room to read some more. I longed to know this God who had His fingerprints all over my life—even through the most difficult times.

## LENNY & PENNY

When I returned from Japan, I wrapped up a few remaining classes necessary to graduate. After graduation in 1984, I needed a place to stay after taking my first real job. I felt God impressing on my heart to call my mother's best friend, "Aunt Penny," the daughter of Grandma and Grandpa Hope. You may recall on the day of my mother's funeral, when Hank took a taxi leaving us orphaned and deserted, Dave called Penny to see if we could live with her. Penny's husband, Bill, was dying of cancer and, as much as she wanted to take us in, she really wasn't in a position to do so. Dave's second choice was to go to the Reils'. The rest is history.

This time, when I called Penny to reconnect after thirteen years, she was thrilled to have me live a couple of months with her and her new husband, Lenny Mitchell. I've always thought God seems to have a thing with names ... Lenny and Penny. Cute. Getting to know Lenny was a blast. I learned that he was a well-known saxophonist during the Big Band era, played with the Tommy Dorsey band, and was a part of creating more than a hundred albums.

Lenny had an exciting career in film and television, too. He was in the original *A Star Is Born* picture with Judy Garland, as the saxophonist. He played the trumpeter in Cecil B. DeMille's epic *The*

*Ten Commandments*. There's a key scene in that film that shows a hand blowing a horn, and Lenny told me a funny story about what it took to get that shot right for the film. It's one of those huge crowd scenes with thousands of people.

Lenny kept ripping out of his costume because it was too tight for him. Keep in mind that Lenny was a bodybuilder. Mr. DeMille would shout, "Okay, Mitchell, get your costume repaired. Take a ten-minute break." Lenny put his watch on to make sure he got back in time. The costume crew stitched him up while thousands of people were waiting for the shot.

Ten minutes later, Mr. DeMille called, "Action." One problem. Lenny forgot to take off his watch. When he put his horn to his lips to sound the trumpet, the director called, "Cut! Mitchell, take your wristwatch off!"

A number of years later, Lenny got a job as the saxophonist for the sixties hit music variety TV show *Shindig!* In spite of his professional successes, Lenny felt something was missing in his life. At the end of one of the *Shindig!* shows, he literally threw his arms up while the camera was panning the stage and said out loud, "God, there has to be more to life than this!" While his comment wasn't heard by the television audience, God was listening. Not long afterward, Lenny's hearing became impaired. He dropped out of performing music, gave his heart to the Lord, and became a music instrument repairman in East Los Angeles.

When Lenny committed his heart to God, he pursued studying the Bible with the same passion that made him a great musician. When I moved in with Lenny and Penny, Lenny was instrumental in cementing my faith in the Lord. He and I sat for three or four hours a day just to study the Bible together and pray. I've never seen someone with such deep convictions. Through Lenny, the Lord was getting a hold of my heart in a deeper way.

Living with Lenny was like enrolling in a crash course in biblical studies, an experience that helped me grow as a Christian young man. Lenny took it upon himself to talk to me about what it meant to be a man, and the importance of living as a person of integrity, honesty, honor, and faithfulness. I never saw these traits in my father. I had much to learn and, thankfully, Lenny was a patient mentor. He knew life was about learning and sometimes it takes time to get it. When it came to the topic of dating, Lenny challenged me to wait on God for the woman I'd one day marry. I wasn't sure how that worked, but I was about to find out.

## THE CHAPEL OF LOVE

I was sitting at a Wednesday-night church service at Lake Arrowhead Christian Fellowship when the pastor stopped his preaching and walked right up to me in the middle of the service. He said, "I have a word from the Lord for you." Me? I looked over my shoulder to make sure he wasn't talking to someone else. "I believe God has your mate picked out for you," he said. "She's going to have a heart for the things of God. She'll be your crown."

I didn't know the pastor well. We weren't friends. I'm not sure if he even knew my name. We'd never talked about my dating life—or lack thereof, since I had stopped dating for some time. In the back of my mind I thought, *I can't come back to this church. It's obviously not a Bible-believing church. I don't think God still sends messages this way these days. Maybe this guy is one of those false prophets the Bible warns about.*

When he finished, the pastor moved on to two or three other

people with a message for them. I thought he was simply stating the obvious. I figured he targeted me since I was twenty-four and didn't have a wedding ring on. I was obviously the eligible bachelor type. I was uncomfortable with the experience and left that evening with no plans of ever returning to the church.

Just three days later on Saturday, I was the best man at the wedding of Dan, a friend I studied with in Japan, and his bride, Tina. Dan told me, "Tina's got a friend I think you'll like. You're both Christians. We think you guys will really hit it off." Evidently, their friend Jean was at the same place I was—neither of us dated. Instead, we were waiting on God. Dan and Tina made a point of introducing us before the night was through.

Shortly after the brief introduction, Jean needed to leave. With no thought of what the pastor had said a few nights earlier, I remember saying to a friend, "I think that's the woman I'm going to marry." Still, I didn't pursue dating her. In fact, it took Dan and Tina nine months to get us to agree to go out with them on a double date, an Amy Grant concert at Pacific Amphitheater in Costa Mesa. That night, as we later learned by comparing notes, we both knew that we were going to marry one another. Isn't that amazing? On August 24, 1986, about a month after I turned twenty-five, Jean and I were married.

While we got off to a wonderful start, married life wasn't always rosy. Marriage is hard work. Both of us had things in our past that threatened to derail us from staying together. One evening we were getting ready for bed and I stepped into the bathroom to brush my teeth. When I came out, Jean was sobbing.

I sat on the edge of the bed next to her and said, "What's up?" "I just don't think you should stay married to me," she replied. I knew she was wrestling with depression, as well as a lack of confidence that she'd be a good mother once we started having children.

Of course, I had the same kinds of questions of my own: whether or not I'd be a good dad since I didn't have a solid example to model.

I slipped my arm around her and said, "Jean, it seems to me that there are only two options for us, because divorce is not an option. We can do marriage one of two ways: happily or unhappily. With all of the stuff that's gone on in my life, I'd much rather do this happily."

That bedrock of commitment sparked a desire in us to get Christian counseling, which ultimately helped untangle the difficulties in our background that kept us from winning at our marriage. That was eighteen years ago. As a result of seeking a marriage counselor, our relationship today is stronger than ever. As of this writing, we've been married twenty years and I can say with certainty that God has blessed us in ways we never dreamed.

## THE BOYS

One of the things I love about my wife is her incredible nurturing heart. I first noticed Jean's innate mothering flair in the way she related to animals. We had five indoor cats and four outdoor cats at one point because Jean would find strays or unwanted kitties who needed love. One cat in particular was partially paralyzed. We called her Little Kitty and loved her as if she were no different from the rest.

When we started discussing having kids, Jean wasn't sure that she was capable of being a good mother. I wanted to have kids, but didn't know if the timing was right. Again, I felt the Lord saying to me, "Jim, don't pressure Jean." About age thirty-eight, Jean had a change of heart. With the window of childbearing closing, and having completed her college course work in biology, she felt it was time. When she came to me and said she was ready to start, I was excited at the chance to be a dad.

Jean had a really long labor with our firstborn son, Trent—upward of twenty hours. When the nurses brought Trent into the birthing center, Jean was understandably exhausted. She needed to sleep. The nurses, however, were trying to make sure that Trent stayed with us that first day as much as possible—part of the bonding process.

I was so captivated by Trent that I literally held him in a rocking chair throughout the night. I never tired of gazing into his precious face or smelling his fresh newborn scent. I prayed over him, thanking the Lord for such a blessing. I asked God for the strength and wisdom to do a better job raising him than my dad did for us. I also prayed that the Lord would take away my fears—my apprehension because I didn't know how to be a dad.

Our second son, Troy, arrived on the scene almost two years later to the day. Both boys were August babies, but if Trent took his time in labor, Troy decided to get a running start. At first, Jean thought she was just having back pain. Like some women, she tended to go into denial when in labor. But at two o'clock in the morning, her water broke.

We lost no time jumping into the car. We strapped Trent in the car seat and I called my sister Dee Dee on the way and asked her to meet us at the hospital. I ran several red lights, fearful that Troy would be born in the front seat.

In the hospital parking lot, Dee Dee and I made a hurried hand-off with Trent, our two-year-old. That done, I raced into the lobby and to the evening nurse's window. Banging on the glass, I called out, "My wife's going to have a baby right now." A woman approached and told me to calm down. She was really taking her time and I was annoyed.

Thankfully, a nurse wheeled Jean in as I dealt with the mountain of paperwork. Moments later, somebody came running out of the birthing room and said, "Mister, if you want to see your baby being born, you'd better get in there." I walked into the room as Troy was being born. They cut the umbilical cord and then the catch nurse took Troy's vital signs at a workstation.

Behind me, I overheard some murmuring from the nurses who had gathered around our baby boy. When I went over to look at Troy, I was told his color was not quite right. When the doctor finished with Jean, he turned and looked at Troy. Within a minute, they whisked him out. Evidently, Troy had ingested a lot of fluid and his lungs were full.

He was taken into the neonatal intensive care unit where he was put on an IV drip. A series of X-rays were taken. For the first forty-eight hours, that poor little guy was poked and pricked and tested to identify why his vital signs were so low. We didn't see him for twenty-four hours, which caused us a great deal of stress. His welcome to the world was very different from Trent's, whom I cuddled in the rocking chair all night. Troy remained on oxygen around the clock for four months to help dry out his lungs. Happily, he turned out to be a suitable match for Trent's boundless energy.

For the last few years, just about every morning, Troy comes into our bedroom at four o'clock to snuggle with us. Troy is one of the cutest little boys on the planet, and Jean and I have to remember that this routine won't last long. When he climbs into our bed, he slips under the covers right next to me and does this little wiggle as he gets cozy. I'll wake up as he settles in and hear his little voice say, "I love you, Daddy." It's the best feeling in the world ... and it reminds me that I'm finally home.

## 14

# Who Would Have Thunk It?

My first big job after college was working in the paper industry. I eventually worked for a division of International Paper, a global giant in the field of paper and packaging products. I was in sales and found myself on a fast track climbing the corporate ladder—not that that was a goal of mine. After a relatively short time on the team, the plant manager took me to lunch at a fancy French restaurant in Berkeley, California, where he offered me a top position with a six-figure salary. I was given several days to consider my decision, which, on the surface, seemed to be a no-brainer.

As a newly married man, things were looking up.

Little did I know that a phone call from an old buddy, who was working with Dr. James Dobson and Focus on the Family, would change my life. He asked me if I would be interested in working in the nonprofit arena, specifically with Focus on the Family's mission to strengthen marriage and families. I had to make a quick decision about my pending promotion at International Paper, and so I took the next plane to Los Angeles for an interview.

Jean and I were big fans of the Focus on the Family broadcast and appreciated Dr. Dobson's insights, so we were somewhat familiar with their mission already. After a day of intense meetings, I was offered a position for one-third of what I was about to make in the paper business. Clearly, money would not be the reason to take this job. Once again, God whispered and, thankfully, my wife and I listened. The decision to work at Focus on the Family placed us on one of the most exciting adventures we could have dreamed of.

My first assignment at Focus on the Family was serving as assistant to the president, Dr. James Dobson. My job was to meet with donors of the ministry around the country to personally thank them for their support and give them an update on the various projects we were undertaking. This was an easy task considering how much I respected the life and work of Dr. Dobson. I have never been around a more gifted individual than Dr. Dobson. He has a keen intellect, loves and is a champion of children of all ages, has incredible integrity, and is deeply committed to his faith in Jesus Christ. Working for him has made my life so much richer.

One of my best experiences was a trip to New York where I met with several players on the Buffalo Bills football team. I had breakfast with free safety Mark Kelso, tight end Pete Metzelaars, and quarterback Frank Reich. I had a great time talking with them about the challenges of playing in the NFL and balancing family life, and thanking them for their support.

Then, for lunch, I was scheduled to meet with a couple who had supported the ministry for a number of years. I called and offered to stop by and pick up sandwiches from a local deli. With lunch in hand, I started out to find their home in a modest neighborhood. As I pulled up, I noticed a ramp leading up to the door. As it turned out, both the husband and wife had been schoolteachers, but several years prior the husband had been in a motorcycle accident and was now confined to a wheelchair.

Over lunch they told us about how they appreciated the work of Focus on the Family and wanted to increase their giving. Up to that point, they had not received any insurance settlement from the accident and gave from what the woman made as a schoolteacher. For me, the day was a picture of how God has wonderful people from all walks of life supporting us. Some are well-known people like the football players, while others are the unsung heroes simply living their lives faithfully and, to the best of their ability, giving to help others.

In 1992, Focus on the Family launched an international division. Because of my studies in Japan, Peb Jackson, then senior vice president over public affairs, felt it would be good to have me assist him, along with a couple of other colleagues, in establishing the new international effort. Dr. Dobson was very concerned about falling into the trap of being too much the ugly American in our work outside of the United States. He wasn't sure the content we created for families would be relevant for our friends overseas and would often remind us not to "push" our way into a country. We were there to serve *if* our resources were a fit.

Peb was a genius at laying out the right approach for the work of the international division. "Only go where local folks have invited us to come and join them," he said. Our first task was to follow up with people who contacted us from places such as South Africa, Australia, New Zealand, Europe, Japan, Korea, Malaysia, and China.

My first exploratory trip to Africa was unforgettable. The people we met were so warm and welcoming. Of particular significance was a lunch with Dr. Lillian Wahome, who was trained in psychology from Kenyatta University in Nairobi, Kenya, and was very familiar with Focus on the Family. As we sat for lunch, I said, "Lillian, do you think our message will resonate with folks in Africa and around the world?"

With a wry smile, she said, "It's just like Americans to think you invented families, because you invent everything! But, if you talk to people about keeping their marriages together and raising healthy kids, you will be relevant in every culture because every culture deals with these issues." She gave us the confirmation we were looking for and her assessment has proven to be true. We now broadcast in over 150 countries and work with dozens of partners around the world.

In 1996, I was promoted to vice president of our international division and, shortly thereafter, became vice president of marketing, concurrently with the international role. I was wearing two hats and working hard. Jean was finishing up her degree in biology/chemistry, and I was completing my masters of business administration. Our household was as busy as a beehive even though the boys hadn't been born yet.

During those years I was struck by the fact that Focus on the Family had an extraordinary amount of great content on a wide range of family-oriented subjects. My challenge was to make families aware of this content. From there, I was promoted into a new role as group vice president and, soon after, became the chief operations officer under Focus on the Family's then-president, Don Hodel, a great man of faith who was the secretary of interior and energy under President Ronald Reagan. Working with Don was a highlight. He's such a gifted person, a man I respect deeply.

He exemplified what it means to be a servant leader and was indispensable in assisting Dr. Dobson as he began the journey transitioning from day-to-day management of Focus on the Family to concentrating on the creative aspect of his work. I was stunned, then, when I learned that Don was stepping down as president of the ministry. I was at a loss for words when Don approached me about filling the role of president.

## YOU'VE GOT THE WRONG GUY

In the summer of 2004, Don took me aside and said, "You know, Jim, I've given this a lot of thought and I've talked with members of the board. We think that you just might be the guy to lead Focus once I step down. Let's see what the Lord does." There was no way this was going to go anywhere, I thought. I mean, I was the guy with no family tree—no grandparents, aunts, uncles, or cousins—and they think I'm the right person to lead a ministry to strengthen families? I don't recall even mentioning the idea to Jean. I do remember saying to the Lord, "Whatever you want to do, that's fine with me. But I just want to continue moving forward in my role serving the best way I know how."

That fall, Don came back to me and said, "Jim, both the board and Dr. Dobson are definitely serious about handing the leadership of the ministry to you. We think it's a great fit." At that point I thought I'd better talk more seriously to Jean about this and we needed to pray.

I came home after work and found Jean doing the dishes at the sink. I'll never forget her reaction when I broke the news to her. She stopped loading the dishes into the dishwasher and said, "Who would have thunk it?" Without skipping a beat, she added a humorous touch by saying, "Can you take out the garbage now?" She has a way of keeping my feet on the ground.

That evening we prayed about what this promotion would mean, especially since at that point we had the two boys to consider. Thankfully, Dr. Dobson shared our concern. He said, "Listen, Jim, your number-one priority is those boys. We've got to make sure if we do this that they are not negatively impacted."

In January 2005, Don and his wife, Barbara, took a much-needed and well-deserved two-week vacation to Hawaii. I remember receiving a phone call from Don on January 10. He explained that he was thinking June would be the right time to announce the transition. The board would be meeting then and formalizing the promotion. He wanted to know if I was comfortable with that timing. "June would be great," I said.

I could almost hear Don smile across the miles when he said, "Well, if June is great, how about the February board meeting?" I felt my heart jump. "Don," I said, "that's like six weeks away!" He said, "Once we make this decision, we've got to just do it because people will start coming to you. Making the move sooner would be cleaner." The rest was history.

On the night before the official "investiture" ceremony in late February, I was restless. I never sought the office of president and I was being asked to fill some rather large shoes. The board wisely divided the responsibilities between the future radio voice and the administrative duties, concluding that it would be difficult to find someone who could juggle both. My primary role would be on the administrative side of the organization. I don't know how Dr. Dobson carried such a heavy load for more than two decades.

You can imagine the doubts I felt when faced with the reality of this new opportunity. Did I have what it took to do the job? Certainly there was nothing in my personal background to suggest I was capable of the position. I didn't come from generations of a strong Christian family tree. I was born into a troubled situation with two alcoholic parents and a father who loved to gamble. My parents' marriage ended in divorce. Why would Dr. Dobson and the board think I could handle so much responsibility?

I remembered Dr. Dobson talking about his grandfather who prayed for him every day even before he was born. Dr. Dobson's father had a remarkable prayer life, too. He was known as the guy who wore out the toes of his shoes before the soles because he was on his knees praying so much. Talk about a rich heritage. I couldn't remember a time when my father prayed.

Dr. Dobson's mother also played an incredible role in his life. He says that many of the parenting and discipline techniques he wrote about in *Dare to Discipline* and *The Strong-Willed Child* weren't from the University of Southern California's Child Development Department from where he graduated. Rather, they came from his mother and what he gleaned from her wisdom over the years, as well as what he'd learned from Scripture.

Humanly speaking, it seemed to me that the right guy for the job should have a similar background. While my own mother did the best she could in raising us, she didn't know God until the end of her life and, therefore, wasn't incorporating the wealth of knowledge that comes from the Bible in her parenting. Yet, she did convey the importance of honesty and treating people right.

With all of these observations churning away in my mind, sleep was difficult. About two o'clock in the morning, I lay in bed and thought, *Lord, You have got the wrong guy. There's been a mistake. My story is on the other end of this continuum. I've experienced so much dysfunction and pain. What do I possibly have to offer?*

I remember the Lord answering me in the quiet of the night. He impressed an amazing message upon my heart: "Jim, get the focus off you because I own it all. This promotion is not about you. As long as you seek Me, I'm in it all. I'll use what was healthy and unhealthy in your life in ways you cannot imagine. Trust Me." That was a profound night for me. And I can honestly say that since then I've felt His presence every step of the way on this exciting journey.

Allow me to offer one other thought. While working on this book, I traveled to Costa Rica to visit the Focus office in the capital city, San Jose. Someone on that trip talking to a large group observed, "The Bible is honest about its heroes. More often than not, it's the brokenhearted people that God uses." There was something in his statement that resonated with me. I'm not suggesting that I'm a hero—rather, that a broken heart is vital to God's work in our lives. You and I can grow and experience good things from God even when we encounter adversity and pain if we are honest about our brokenness.

On my way back from that trip, as I reflected on this unexpected turn of events in my life, I was struck by something I had read in the Bible. Time and again, God uses the foolish things of this world to confound the wise. Here's the nugget in my view. In spite of how desperate one's circumstances are, God is still in the business of healing our brokenness and, like a gifted surgeon, He takes the pieces of our lives and makes us whole once again.

I am convinced that no matter how torn up the road has already been, or how pothole-infested the road may look ahead, nothing—*nothing*—is impossible for God. In the words of Jesus, "With man this is impossible, but with God all things are possible" (Matthew 19:26).

I know. I'm living proof.

15

# Reflections on Faith and Family

I have a confession to make.

There are a host of "life lessons" that I could offer to you based upon my journey: living with Dad and Mom, their divorce, Mom's remarriage, her death, Hank's leaving, becoming an orphan, living with the Reils, reuniting with Dad, his death, and my coming to faith thanks to the role of a godly mentor in my life. So much could be said.

However, I'm not entirely comfortable giving advice, primarily because I see myself as a fellow traveler, not an "expert" on family life. My hesitation comes from the recognition that my story is just that—my story. The details are different from yours. I don't want to put God into a box by suggesting that He will work the same way in your life as He has in mine. What I *can* say with certainty is that *God is near to those who hurt.* As King David, who had his share of distress, wrote in the Psalms, "The LORD is close to the brokenhearted and saves those who are crushed in spirit" (34:18).

Being broken is very real to me. I think it's a good state for the human heart to be in—at least for a season. I've found that when I am broken, I can finally understand how totally dependent I am on

God. Sometimes I wonder whether we make a mistake when we try to save others or ourselves from experiencing brokenness—as if having a broken spirit was like having the plague. Our culture is bent on experiencing "happiness" and being "pain-free" no matter what the cost. In fact, if the truth were known, billions of dollars are spent annually just medicating pain in our society.

Certainly it's tempting to mask our pain—whether physical, relational, emotional, or spiritual—through distractions: entertainment, work, and sports. Pain hurts, and who wants that? Yet, in spite of our best efforts to avoid brokenness, for many people, it seems to be a prerequisite for coming to a relationship with God. I know that was the case for me.

What's more, the purpose of pain is often to develop our character, yet we run from it because pain is the gift that nobody wants. I believe that we rarely understand or perhaps overlook the benefits that pain can bring, not the least of which are the qualities of patience, obedience, and dependence on God.

Which is why I've set aside the airbrush. I've wanted to be open with you about the failures, shortcomings, and trials I've encountered as well as the amazing way God redeemed my trail of brokenness. Truly, He has fashioned the splintered pieces of my life into a remarkable mosaic. It is my prayer, then, that you come away from my story with a picture of hope … even when your circumstances look bleak. As Paul, another follower of Jesus, wrote, "And we know that in all things God works for the good of those who love him" (Romans 8:28).

That said, before passing along a few observations about faith and family, let me be clear about one other thing: I didn't relate the details of my story to elicit sympathy. I know I'm not the only person who has lived and suffered under the same roof with alcoholic parents—nor will I be the last. Our mailbag at Focus on the Family yields letters every day from those whose stories are just as compelling as mine—if not more so. Stories where the sting of hurt and feelings of betrayal run deep, and where hope has run dry.

Every time I read one of those letters, I want to pick up the phone and say, "I understand a little of what you may be feeling." I want to remind those who are living in desperate circumstances that their file hasn't blown off God's desk. Their marriages may be on the rocks, their kids may be out of control, but He still knows where they live. He cares for them in spite of what they may think at the moment.

God has both the power to quiet our storms and the ability to give our lives new meaning and purpose. Again, those are not empty words. I've lived them and know that nothing is impossible for God. As the prophet Jeremiah wrote, "I am the LORD, the God of all mankind. Is anything too hard for me?" (32:27).

I've had several decades to process the events of my life, and believe there are a few nuggets of truth you may find beneficial. Probably a good place to start is by sharing an important observation that I've only recently grasped: When I was born, I had no control over who my parents would be or over the choices they'd make. In other words, *I'm not responsible for the behavior of my parents.*

I could have been born into a home where my parents were wealthy or poor. My dad and mom could have been the king and queen of some faraway land. Dad could have been the governor of California, or a window washer in New York City. It was liberating when I realized that my parents were who they were and I had nothing to do with their lot in life. I wasn't even born when they chose to turn to alcohol for comfort.

What's more, I had no control over what occurred in my parents' history. I had nothing to do with the influences, the friends, the circumstances, or the choices that shaped them into the mother and father they became. Their ideas of parenting and discipline, spending and saving, fidelity and integrity, financial management and debt, were all shaped long before I arrived on the scene.

That's profound. Why?

Once again, *I'm not responsible for the behavior of my parents.* I know this now as an adult. When I was young, however, such insight flew way over my head as it typically does for children. Far too many of the problems we struggle with as adults can be traced back to the thought that we were somehow responsible for the actions of our parents. If they divorced, we tend to blame ourselves. If they drank to excess, we think we must have done something to cause them to medicate with alcohol.

Nothing could be further from the truth.

When I say that I am not responsible for my parents' behavior, that's not to say that I'm unaffected by their choices. I was … and I am. At the same time, as I've said, God owns it all. While I may not understand what I experienced as a result of how my parents acted, He knows what's going on and He cares. Nothing that happened in my life took Him by surprise.

Put another way, to paraphrase one of my favorite verses in the Bible: Right now we see through the glass dimly. We see in part. We know in part. But we press on because one day all will become clear (1 Corinthians 13:12). I don't know the big picture. I don't have all of the facts. God is at work—for good—even when I cannot make sense out of life's circumstances. If I fail to grasp this, it's easy for me to think of myself as a *victim* of what my parents did instead of a *vessel* loved by God.

My desire is to be God's vessel, to be used by Him as He sees fit. God allowed me to grow up in a home where my dad was betting the farm on the ponies and addicted to the bottle, as well as a household where my mother was a single-parent recovering alcoholic struggling to raise five kids. Why? I can't say for sure. Meanwhile, I've decided to resist the temptation to play the part of a victim and, instead, seek to be His vessel.

When I say vessel, I mean someone who chooses to allow God to use their pain for His glory, for His purposes, for what He knows is best. Will I ever be a "perfect" vessel? No, not even close. This side of heaven the warts and wrinkles of life are part of the experience. But, with His help I can become more like Him.

## PROMISES, PROMISES

One of the more poignant examples of the pain I felt as a result of my dad's poor choices was the day he promised to bring me a baseball mitt and didn't follow through. His failure has had a profound impact on me. Yes, I was saddened and hurt by his choice. I wish my memories of that exchange had a happy ending. I'd like to think that my dad had a perfectly good reason for failing to keep such a big promise to his seven-year-old son.

But he didn't.

On a positive note, his failure taught me, now that I'm a dad, to be extra careful with the promises I make to the boys. Allow me a personal example. Several months ago I was feeling a great deal of pressure. Things at the office were intense. The ministry was going through a restructuring to better serve our constituents. The changes were needed but sometimes tricky to implement without stepping on toes during the shuffle.

Meanwhile, Jean and I were moving across town to give the boys a little more leg room to climb trees and play in the dirt. With the sale of one home, the purchase of another, packing fifteen years of stuff, not to mention the responsibilities at work, I was feeling a lot of stress. Not to make excuses, but living out of boxes and eating fast food off paper plates, while trying to juggle the rest of life, shortened my fuse day by day.

Conditions were right for the perfect storm, and it hit.

In meltdown moments like these, I confess I can lose my cool as fast as the next guy—especially when the kids go haywire. Jean is such a gift. She privately and lovingly pointed out that my barking at the kids wasn't the best way to deal with their misbehavior. She was right. If I wasn't careful, my words and my tone could pound away on my kids with the same damaging forcefulness as the ball-peen hammer my father used that night at the "hammer house." Bellowing out orders, demanding obedience, and speaking in strident tones can just as easily wound the spirit of my children as the rants of a raving drunk.

By God's grace, I decided the hammering would stop here with me. Since my tone was clearly affecting Trent, our five-year-old, I sat with him in his bedroom and said, "Trent, I love you and I want to make you a promise."

That got his attention.

You see, the boys and I had talked on a previous occasion about the topic of promise keeping. I've pointed them to what Jesus said in Matthew 5:37: "Simply let your 'Yes' be 'Yes,' and your 'No,' 'No.'" In other words, I explained, we're supposed to stand by our promises; we're to say what we mean and mean what we say. While they don't know about the story of my dad's failure to keep his promise, my boys knew by my direct look and tone of voice that making a *promise* was a big deal.

I asked, "Trenton, are you ready?" He nodded. "My promise, Trent, is that I'm not going to speak with anger toward you. It's a tough promise to make and I know I'll feel angry in spite of my efforts to stick to that promise. So, here's the deal. When I start to get angry, I want you to hold me accountable and remind me of my promise. Will you?"

He thought about that for a moment, and then said, "Sure, Dad." Of course, as part of our little talk, I walked through the difference between being *stern* and being *angry*, but committing to throttle my anger was an attempt to connect with him and build trust between us. I believe it helped him grasp the importance of making, and keeping, a promise.

Sometime later, Trent was giving his mother a difficult time. Frankly, the infraction was probably some silly thing that boys find funny but adults find annoying. I took him aside to the living room and said, "Trent, I need you to make a promise to me. I need you to promise that you'll treat Mommy better today when she speaks to you, okay?"

There was an extended silence as Trent considered the commitment he was being asked to make. After a moment, he looked at me and said, "Okay, Dad. I'll make you that promise." Remembering stories like these gives me hope when I begin to doubt myself and wonder how anything good could possibly come from the kind of messed-up childhood I experienced.

I've been keeping a beautiful, leather-bound journal for each of my boys. My first entry predated their births. I plan to give them their personal journal when they turn sixteen. Not only have I written thoughts and observations about their unique lives, I've included maps from all over the world where I've traveled, and taped in money from foreign countries. Photos from their early life and, most importantly, observations about their spiritual journey round out the journal.

For example, in an entry dated March 26, 2006, in Trent's book, I recorded a touching moment when Trent, Troy, and I were kicking a beach ball around in a large, darkened room. Troy, who was three at the time, announced, "Daddy, I'm afraid of the dark." Without hesitation, five-year-old Trent put his arm around his younger brother and said, "Just get closer to God, Troy, and you won't be afraid of the dark."

The tenderness of Trent's heart as well as his love of God displayed in that precious exchange are further evidence that God's Spirit is restoring my past. He is redeeming those days of brokenness for His purposes right now as well as for the benefit of generations to come.

## LET 'EM EAT CAKE

You and I have a choice to make and a message to send. We can repeat the mistakes made by our parents or we can take the best of what we've learned from them, reject the baggage, and choose to set a new course for ourselves and for our families. Each day the decisions you and I make can communicate to those we love that there's nothing we'd rather do than to *be there* for them.

That's so important for me, as a dad, to remember. I'll admit it's easy to slip into the role of the House Disciplinarian—you know, Keeper of the Peace, and Enforcer of the Rules. It's much more difficult for a tapped-out parent to dream up hands-on, creative ways to encourage horseplay and laughter in the home. Yet, like rain and sunshine, both discipline and play are needed for our kids to thrive and to know that we're crazy about them.

As I learned from my mother, laughter is one of the best ways of communicating love, affection, and nurturing a sense of well-being. She found endless ways of lifting our spirits in spite of our circumstances. Thanks to her easygoing example, I've learned to take life as it comes. I really don't stress out about things. In fact, I usually find humor to be good medicine for the soul.

Speaking of creating a festive mood in the home, I've heard of a family that every Friday evening conducts what they call "Barbarian Night." Typically, something really messy is served—like spaghetti and meatballs with plenty of sauce. The plates, silverware, and napkins are locked away. Everyone, including Mom and Dad, must eat barbarian-style: that's *fingers only* and right off of the plastic tablecloth.

Their kids absolutely love it. The laughter and downright ridiculous memories created by that weekly mess far outweigh the extra cleanup involved. Maybe an idea like that appeals to you. Then again, you might opt for something less messy, like "Upside-down Day" where dinner and breakfast trade places. I know that Jean and I want to do whatever we can to make our house a home where there's no shortage of good times, surprises, and laughter.

For those of us with children, I really believe that *now* is the time to start filling the memory banks of our kids with generous deposits of fun, love, and screams of joy. And, whether or not you have kids, consider the youth in your neighborhood who may not have a mom or dad. Maybe find a creative way to put a smile on their face too.

I think I might just stop by the store tonight in time for dinner to pick up some spaghetti and meatballs ... and serve them barbarian-style.

The boys will be thrilled!

## GOD IS STILL IN CONTROL

There are a number of people in my life whom I could harbor tremendous bitterness toward, including my dad, Hank, and Mr. Reil. However, if I were to take what they did to me and drag it around like a ball and chain of resentment, guess who would still be in jail? Me. But, as I forgive them and when I don't attempt to "own" any of the destructive decisions or actions they made toward me, then I'm free. I don't have to live my life peering into the rearview mirror. In fact, I feel stronger when I release what was done to me. How? The space in my heart that had been preoccupied with anger or hurt can be set aside to make room for a joy and a peace that makes no sense whatsoever—because God promises that gift to the brokenhearted.

In addition to the fact that I am not responsible for the behavior of my parents, that I have a choice to be a victim or a vessel, that God owns it all, that keeping promises is so important, and making my home a place where love and laughter are celebrated, there's another key insight worth mentioning. You might think what I'm about to say is obvious. However, so often we lose sight of the simple truth that the world we live in is a broken place: *This life is not always the way God intended life to be.*

Far too often, we maintain expectations that are unrealistic for a fallen world. We forget that life is not perfect, and we become surprised, even hurt and disillusioned, when things don't work out perfectly. We're stunned when they don't work out at all. We make the mistake of buying into the concept that, if we do certain things, then God, like a cosmic genie, will bless us or make our situation more comfortable, painless, or acceptable as defined by our misguided standards.

Unfortunately, living in the United States tends to give us a distorted picture of life. Most of us *are* blessed with creature comforts. We have food to eat. Cars to drive. A roof over our heads. The idea that we must eliminate all pain is unrealistic, yet we continue to set the bar so high that we forget that life is tough for everyone at some point. Trials will come and we need clarity in order to face them.

The death of my mother, for instance, was one of the most difficult watershed moments in my life. Looking back, I wish someone had taken me aside, put their arm around me, and given me some honest perspective about the brokenness of this fallen world. Maybe something along these lines:

*Jimmy, difficult things like the death of a parent happen to all of us. When we lose someone we love, the pain and despair we feel can be overwhelming at times. No matter what you encounter in life, remember that this life isn't the end. There's a new heaven and a new earth ahead awaiting you. That's what God promises. In the meantime, don't let sadness or bitterness consume you. If, when you wake up all you can do is put one foot in front of the other, then do that much. Trust God for the courage to face the new day and to lead the way.*

At least that's what I, as a nine-year-old, needed to hear.

At times, I still need those words.

Perhaps, in times of trials, the most realistic thing you and I can do is to pray, "Lord, just help me to keep standing at the end of all this mess."

I was driving to work the other day reflecting on these thoughts when the song "Cry Out to Jesus," by the Christian music group Third Day, filled the speakers. I immediately resonated with the honesty and perspective of their lyrics. They sang:

When you're lonely, and it feels like
the whole world is falling on you.
You just reach out, you just cry out to Jesus.
Cry to Jesus
To the widow who suffers from being alone

Wipin' the tears from her eyes
And for the children around who are without a home
Say a prayer tonight
There is hope for the hopeless, rest for the weary
And love for the broken heart
There is grace and forgiveness, mercy and healing
He'll meet you wherever you are

Yes, life is hard. There is adversity. While seasons of smooth sailing do occur, more often than not, life feels like it's coming apart at the seams. Rather than hide our pain in order to preserve our pride, I believe it's time to take off our masks and be open with one another about the brokenness that we all experience. After all, isn't that the example Jesus Himself set for us as He faced the prospect of dying on the cross?

Hours before Jesus was betrayed by one of His close friends to be crucified, He was praying and weeping and baring His soul to God the Father. Jesus, who lived a sinless life was, in that moment, faced with the prospect of carrying our sins while being mocked and vilified by a horde of bloodthirsty Roman soldiers and hypocritical religious leaders. More than that, He knew when the sins of the world were placed upon His shoulders, God the Father would have to break fellowship with Him for a season.

No wonder Jesus asked the question: "My God, My God, why have you forsaken me?" (Mark 15:34).

You see, throughout His earthly life, Jesus experienced a daily intimacy with God that eclipses our ability to fathom. Given that Jesus was both fully God and fully man, the prospect of a separation from God would literally tear apart His heart. Believe it or not, this is encouraging to me. Why? Because of the suffering of Jesus, I can be 100 percent positive that He understands exactly what you and I feel when we reach the end of our rope.

If Jesus wasn't afraid to ask, "My God, why have You left me?" then you and I are free to be boldly honest and broken before a God who understands what we're experiencing. God isn't insecure. He won't run into the next room fuming about being misunderstood by His children. Rather, He promises to be a friend to the brokenhearted.

Incidentally, this was a big reason I agreed to share my life with you in this book. When we are transparent, we're in the best position to encourage one another to experience the richness and depth of the life God has for us. When we allow God to be involved in our pain, He has this uncanny ability to make sure none of it is wasted.

# Acknowledgments

There are so many people who have helped me catch the meaning of the events that shaped my life. At the front of the line are my siblings, Mike, Dave, Dee Dee, and Kim, who each in their own way provided balance in my unbalanced world. Thank you. To Jean, my wife, who has stood with me for more than twenty years as my better half. You have taught me many things about kindness and love. And to my boys, Trent and Troy, although still young, you provide me lessons every day about life and the joy of being a father.

To my colleagues at Focus on the Family, you are the arms around so many hurting people each day. Well done! Dr. James Dobson, thank you for showing me what it means to be a man who stands up for those who cannot stand for themselves. You are a father to so many wounded sons and daughters.

To Cris Doornbos, Andrea Christian, and the entire team at David C. Cook, thank you for believing this story might help someone find meaning, hope, and salvation in Jesus Christ. Your faith and confidence in my story completes a journey that started so many years ago.

Bob DeMoss, my friend for twenty years, I want to thank you for the many hours trying to get the story just right. Your talent has made this book far better than it would have been. And to Greg Johnson, my agent, someone who knows the quiet pain of a wounded spirit, your help has been immeasurable.

To those who read the manuscript and provided invaluable insight into how the story flowed. These friends include Glenn and Natalie Williams, Dan and Susie Rieple, Gillian Sanguinetti, Becky Wilson, Dr. and Mrs. DeMoss, and Leticia DeMoss.

To the countless people who showed me kindness along the way.

Often it was someone with a word of encouragement or a hug. Especially, to my teachers and coaches that modeled what is good and true in those early years. Thank you for caring!

Finally, to the Lord who promised to be a father to the fatherless. Thank you for taking the broken pieces of my life and weaving them into an amazing picture of Your grace.

## About the Author

After pursuing careers in sales and international business, Jim Daly became a member of the Focus on the Family team in 1989. Since then he has risen through the organization until becoming president and CEO in 2005. He lives with his wife of twenty years, Jean, and their two sons, in Colorado Springs.

For more information about Focus on the Family's resources, visit www.Family.org, or call toll free: 1-800-A-FAMILY (800-232-6459).